New Trea
Of English

3

Grammar
Comprehension
Creative writing

Editor Francis Connolly

Design Philip Ryan

Illustration: Jane Golden

Artwork Frinzi Ryan & Associates

Type origination EC Typesetting. Set in Garamond.

ISBN 1 85276019 2

© Folens Ltd. London 1988.
Printed by Folens Publishers, Dublin.

Contents

New Treasury of English 3

New Treasury of English is a core scheme that aims to introduce children to the salient features of English grammar. The series develops their ability to comprehend written passages and utilises both grammar and comprehension in a series of relevant and structured exercises. The passages have been carefully chosen to give a wide variety of interesting material drawn from both fact and fiction.

How the books are constructed

Comprehension. The passages are of varying length and complexity. The child is asked a series of questions. In some cases the answers are explicit in the passage while in others they are implicit. Some questions go beyond the confines of the passage and draw on the pupil's more general experience and skills. In addition there are a number of exercises that are designed specifically to encourage children to look for meaning in writing rather than merely to decode words.

Grammar. The only grammar introduced is that which will enhance the child's style of writing and speech. Grammar is not treated as an end in itself; technical names for parts of speech, for example, are not used at this level. Each point is introduced by a brief explanation and followed by several sets of reinforcement and consolidation exercises.

Written style. In each book there are several sections that aim to broaden and develop pupil's written style. These vary from drawing attention to over-used words and suggesting alternatives to extending sentence construction. In this book we concentrate on broadening the child's written vocabulary through a series of structured exercises.

How to use these books

Each book contains more work than you are likely to need in one school year. You will probably need to be selective by either concentrating on one particular aspect of the book, say grammar or style or by deciding that it is not necessary for the pupils to complete every exercise. The comprehension passages, in particular, lend themselves to a number of differing approaches. They can certainly be used by the individual child but they can also be used by groups of children, thus providing the basis for useful discussion. They could also be used as completely oral exercises. By starting with some of the shorter passages you could provide a progressive course in listening skills.

The observation of nature and the passage of the seasons provide the major linking theme throughout the book and you may find it useful to use this material to stimulate direct observational work of the children's own environment. Perhaps they could keep an illustrated nature diary.

Whatever you decide to do, you will find that **New Treasury of English,** as well as providing a core scheme, enables you, the teacher, to achieve a high degree of flexibility of approach.

Fact File

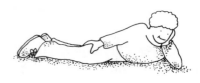

Write this into your book. Fill in the blanks.

My name is ....
I am .... years old.
My address is ....
....
....

I am .... tall. I have .... eyes.
I weigh .... I have .... hair.
There are .... people in my family.
Their names are ....
....
....

My School
I attend .... (school).
The school address is ....
....
....

I am in .... class.
My teacher's name is ....
There are .... pupils in the class.
My favourite subject is ....

My best friends.
1. ....
2. ....
3. ....

My favourite hobbies.
1. ....
2. ....
3. ....

My favourite food.
1. ....
2. ....
3. ....

My favourite T.V. programmes.
1. ....
2. ....
3. ....

Nature Notes For September

SEPTEMBER IS THE MONTH WHEN BLACKBERRIES BEGIN TO RIPEN. WASPS AND BIRDS CAN GET AT THE FRUIT EASILY.

BUT THE JUICIEST BLACKBERRIES SEEM TO BE JUST TOO HIGH UP ON THE BUSH FOR US TO PICK!

THIS IS A HARD TIME FOR THE LITTLE FIELD MOUSE. THE FARMER HAS CUT THE CORN WHERE THE MOUSE HAS BUILT HIS NEST, SO HE HAS NOWHERE TO HIDE FROM THE CATS AND STOATS WHEN THEY HUNT HIM.

LOOK OUT FOR THE RED ADMIRAL BUTTERFLY AT THIS TIME OF THE YEAR. RED ADMIRALS LOVE THE FLOWERS OF THE THISTLE AND IVY.

HERE IS A LEAF FROM A SYCAMORE TREE. DO YOU KNOW IF THERE IS A SYCAMORE TREE NEAR WHERE YOU LIVE?

Nature Quiz

1. When are blackberries ripe?
2. Where do they grow?
3. Name four birds that eat berries.
4. Name four kinds of fruit used to make jam.
5. What colour is a wasp?
6. Where does the wasp live?
7. How does he protect himself?
8. What should you do if you get a sting from a wasp?
9. What is a young butterfly called?
10. How many wings has a butterfly?
11. Where do you see ivy growing?
12. Where does the field mouse build his nest?
13. What enemies has he?
14. What is made from wheat?
15. Where does the sycamore tree have its seed-box?

A 'WHIZZER' LIKE THIS REALLY HOLDS THE SEED OF A SYCAMORE TREE, THE SEEDS WILL SOON COME TWISTING DOWN

Capital Letters

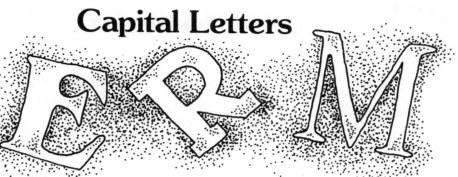

Always begin a sentence with a capital letter.

(A) Write out these sentences, putting in the capital letters.

1. the huge bear wandered into the town.
2. one day he caught a salmon in the river.
3. she asked the young boy to go to the shops.
4. patrick was taken prisoner and brought to Ireland.
5. we were stranded on the island for two days.
6. a crowd of people stood and stared.
7. our pet dog is five years old.
8. the two horses passed the winning post.

Capital letters are used for the names of people and the titles of people:

(B) Write out these sentences, putting in the capital letters.

1. frank byrne is the captain of our team.
2. the winner of the gold medal was susan brown.
3. doctor dolittle was kind to the animals.
4. the prime minister met the president at the airport.
5. kevin and brian went fishing with uncle vincent.
6. we met doctor daly at the hospital.
7. the soldiers were led into the valley by general custer.
8. king john ruled wisely for many years.

(C) Rewrite the following to make sentences, making sure to insert capital letters where necessary.

1. anne swim went morning this for a with joan.
2. found a paul nest garden his in front.
3. lovely done painting that was patricia by.
4. brought injured we boy doctor smith to the.
5. pat hat helen's the on road found.
6. army into led the captain carter battle.
7. bull crowd the frightened angry charged through the.
8. witch spell cast the children the on evil a.

King Of The Trees

I am a mighty oak tree and king of the forest. My thick trunk is hundreds of years old. My roots can split rocks and concrete.

Can you keep a secret? I was once a tiny brown acorn sitting in a pretty egg-cup. One night the wind came and shook me loose from my mother's arms. I hit the ground with a *thud*, tumbled out of my little egg-cup and rolled into a dark hole in the ground. By morning I was covered with a blanket a soft leaves. All that day I lay there, lonely and hungry. Next morning, Polly, the black cow, came and placed her hoof on top of my head. She crushed me deep down into the soft earth.

A few days later something wonderful happened. I began to send tiny hair-roots down into the soil. They supplied me with food and water during the long winter.

I was so delighted when spring came that I pushed small green shoots above the ground. The warm sun and soft rain helped me to grow upwards. My roots were now strong and deep. They fed my growing body. Indeed, I was the happiest *sapling* in the *grove*. The brown hare could no longer jump over my *slender* body. How I longed to be as tall and as strong as my mother and look out over the forest.

As the years passed, I grew bigger and stronger. Birds and squirrels came and built their nests in my strong branches. A fairy ring of toadstools made its home around the base of my trunk.

The next time you go for a walk in the forest stop and look at my *sturdy* trunk. Long before your great-great-grandparents were alive I was king of the forest.

Look up the words in italics in the dictionary at the back of the book. Write down the meaning of each word.

Questions

1. How old is the oak tree?
2. How did the acorn fall?
3. How was the acorn crushed?
4. In what way does the hair-root help the tree?
5. When did the green shoots appear?
6. What would you find at the base of the tree?
7. What is the difference between a grove, a wood and a forest?
8. Fill in the following:
   The king of the jungle is the ....
   The king of the birds is the ....

The Correct Word

(A) Choose the most suitable word in brackets.

1. A horse has four *(hooves, paws, wings)*.
2. A horse has a *(horn, trunk, mane)*.
3. A young horse is called a *(calf, kitten, foal)*.
4. A horse has a coat of *(wool, hair, fur)*.
5. A horse is bigger than a *(giraffe, whale, foal)*.
6. A horse has no *(teeth, whiskers, tail)*.
7. A horse *(sings, barks, neighs)*.
8. A horse's home is called a *(kennel, stable, sty)*.
9. A horse has a long *(ear, tail, nose)*.
10. A horse eats *(soap, hay, stones)*.

(B) Choose the right word in brackets.

1. A swan has a coat of white *(hair, feathers, skin)*.
2. A swan has two *(tails, necks, wings)*.
3. A swan's beak is *(blue, red, yellow)*.
4. A swan *(croaks, hisses, barks)*.
5. A swan is a graceful *(fish, animal, bird)*.
6. A swan has a long *(tail, neck, ear)*.
7. A swan has webbed *(wings, beak, feet)*.
8. A swan cannot *(fly, swim, talk)*.

(C) Underline the correct word in brackets.

1. A lion has four *(hooves, tusks, paws)*.
2. A lion *(barks, roars, bellows)*.
3. A lioness has no *(tail, mane, claws)*.
4. A lion is smaller than an *(ant, elephant, otter)*.
5. A young lion is called a *(puppy, kitten, cub)*.
6. A lion cannot *(swim, leap, fly)*.
7. A lion lives in a *(coop, hole, den)*.
8. A lion has a covering of *(skin, wool, spines)*.

(D) The Cat Family. The following animals are members of the cat family. The letters of their names are jumbled. Write them out correctly.

1. ilno 2. gtrei 3. dlproae 4. hheecta 5. rgjaau 6. xynl 7. muap 8. nhprtea.

The Mermaid Princess

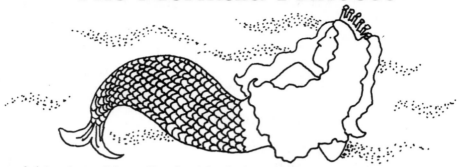

Enda and his sister Nora lived with their mother at the foot of an oval-shaped mountain.

One sunny evening Enda killed a hawk that was about to *pounce* on a singing thrush. The happy bird thanked the children for saving its life and sang sweetly for them.

Just as the thrush was finishing its song, nine fairy pipers appeared. Enda and Nora were delighted. They followed the pipers up the mountainside. The tiny pipers led them to the edge of a golden beach. There they met a kind man on a white horse. He brought them under the sea to Fairyland. They wondered at the underwater world, full of strange *creatures*.

At last they met Miranda, the beautiful mermaid princess. She brought them to her palace. The children were given a royal feast in the great hall. After the feast the fairies played a sweet tune on their pipes. The two children fell into a deep sleep. They slept for seven years. When they awoke Enda was a handsome young man and Nora was a beautiful young woman.

Before they left the palace the princess gave them gifts of gold and silver to bring home. The fairy pipers led them back across the sea and down the oval-shaped mountainside. The children were happy to be home again. When they looked around they saw the wee folk disappearing into a white cloud of mist. Enda and Nora ran towards their mother who was overjoyed to see her long-lost children.

Look up the words in italics in the dictionary at the back of the book. Write down the meaning of each word.

Questions

1. Why did Enda kill the hawk?
2. Where did the pipers lead the children?
3. Where did the kind man bring them?
4. Who was Miranda?
5. What gifts did Miranda give them?
6. Where did the children's mother live?
7. Write down what you think the mother said to her long-lost children when she saw them again.
8. Write what you think the children might have said in reply to their mother.

Larry Long Ears

There was once a king in Wales called Larry Long Ears. He always wore a hooded cloak because he did not want anyone to know that he had horse's ears. Once a year he had his long, golden hair cut. Every barber who cut the king's hair was afterwards put to death, so that he could not tell the king's secret.

One Christmas the king chose a young barber named Jones to cut his hair. Jones was the only son of a poor *widow*. When his mother heard the sad news she went at once to the king's palace. She knelt before King Larry.

"Oh! Please do not kill my only son, your majesty," she begged.

"Since it is Christmas time I will not kill him," said the king.

Jones cut King Larry's hair and promised never to tell anyone about the King's strange secret.

When the young man went home he did not tell the secret to his mother. Soon afterwards Jones began to dream about King Larry's long ears. He became very sick and could not sleep or eat. His mother thought he was going to die. She sent for a wise druid to come and cure him.

"You will never get well until you tell the secret that is troubling you," said the old druid as he laid his hands on Jones' head. "You must walk along the high road until you come to a crossroads. There you will see a stream with a beautiful willow tree growing beside it. Tell your secret to the tree and you will be cured."

Jones did as he was told. He travelled along the dusty road and came to the stream. There he saw the tall willow tree. He laid his head against the tree trunk and whispered his secret to the willow. At once he felt happy and ran home to tell his mother the good news.

Sometime later, the king's *musician* broke his harp. He searched everywhere for the wood of a willow tree to make a new harp. At last he found a willow tree by a stream. He cut down the tree and made a beautiful harp from the soft wood.

That night there was a big feast in King Larry's palace. All the *nobles* and lords were in the great hall. The king ordered his harper to play some music for his guests. But when the harper *plucked* the strings, the harp began to sing loudly:

"King Larry has the ears of a horse ..... the ears of a horse."

There was silence in the great hall. The harper was afraid but King Larry only laughed, took off his hood, and showed everyone his long ears. All the nobles laughed and never again was any barber afraid to cut the king's hair.

Look up the words in italics in the dictionary at the back of the book. Write down the meaning of each word.

Questions

1. What was the name of the story?
2. Why did the king wear a hood?
3. What colour hair had he?
4. What happened to the barbers who cut his hair?
5. Who was Jones?
6. Why did the king spare his life?
7. What promise did Jones make to the king?
8. Why did the young man become sad and silent?
9. Whom did Jones's mother ask to cure him?
10. What did the druid tell Jones to do?
11. How did Jones feel after telling the secret to the tree?
12. Why did the harper cut down the willow tree?
13. Where did the musician play the new harp?
14. What happened as he played the harp?
15. What did the king do?

Creative Writing

A New Pet

1. **Write a story:**

Helpful Words and Ideas

.... birthday .... auntie arrived .... surprise ....
present .... fluffy, white rabbit .... cute and cuddly ....
friendly and playful .... overjoyed .... named it ....
built a hutch .... soft straw .... water .... feed of lettuce and carrots
.... nibbled (took small bites) happily .... clean out each day ....
playing in the back garden .... hopping and skipping .... take good care of
....

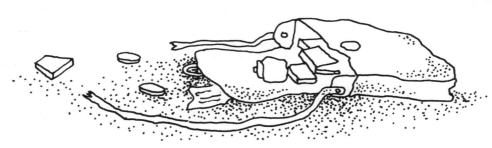

The Stolen Money

2. **Write a story about how you recovered a bag of stolen money and handed it over to the police.**

Helpful Words and Ideas

.... in the park .... playing 'hide and seek' .... hidden in a bush
.... sound of footsteps .... whispers .... a pair of mean-looking men
.... the first man was .... and wore .... the second man
.... a brown bag .... scared stiff .... as quiet as a ....
as still as a .... stuffed the bag under .... hurried away ....
waited a moment .... crept .... pulled out the bag ....
opened .... thousands of pounds .... police station .... reward ....

13

Nature Notes for October

IN OCTOBER, THE LEAVES ARE BEGINNING TO FALL AND ALREADY THE LANES AND WOODS ARE COVERED WITH A CARPET OF BROWN AND GOLD. THE SQUIRREL IS BUSY GATHERING NUTS TO STORE FOR THE WINTER. SOMETIMES THE SILLY SQUIRREL FORGETS WHERE HE HAS HIDDEN THE NUTS!

THIS IS THE LEAF OF A HORSE-CHESTNUT TREE. WE KNOW A HORSE CHESTNUT AS A 'CONKER'

HOUSE-MARTINS AND SWALLOWS FLY OFF TO FIND A WARMER CLIMATE. THEY WILL RETURN AGAIN IN THE SPRING TIME.

THE PRICKLY SEED-HOLDER OF THE CHESTNUT FALLS OFF THE TREE AND BURSTS OPEN.

INSIDE, IN THE SMOOTH LINING LIES A LOVELY SHINY, BROWN CONKER.

THE HEDGEHOG LOOKS OUT FOR A DISUSED RABBIT HOLE WHERE HE CAN MAKE A COSY NEST OF MOSS AND LEAVES. THERE HE SLEEPS DURING THE COLD WEATHER.

Nature Quiz

1. What colours are the autumn leaves?
2. Name six animals that have furry coats.
3. Give another name for a 'conker'.
4. What are conkers used for?
5. Where does the swallow usually build its nest?
6. Why has the swallow strong wings?
7. Where would you see flocks of swallows?
8. What food does the swallow like to eat?
9. How do you think the hedgehog got its name?
10. Why has it spines?
11. What food does it like to eat?
12. Where does the kingfisher live?
13. Why, do you think, is it called a kingfisher?
14. What colour is it?
15. Why has it a long, sharp beak?

YOU MAY BE LUCKY ENOUGH TO SEE THE BEAUTIFUL KINGFISHER PERCHED ON A TREE BY A STREAM, LOOKING OUT FOR FISH TO CATCH.

Capital Letters

Always write I with a capital letter when on its own.

(A) Write out these sentences, putting in the capital I when on its own.

1. i visited the zoo yesterday.
2. Anne and i will call for you at six.
3. i asked if i could go to the cinema.
4. i was annoyed because i was very late.
5. Patrick and i went fishing with Uncle Jim.
6. i always do my homework when i arrive home.
7. If i were you, i would sell the bike.
8. i hope i will be able to visit you soon.

Capital letters are used for the names of the days, the months and special days.

(B) Write out these sentences, putting in the capital letters.

1. i will be ten years of age next february.
2. The farmer brought in the hay at the end of august.
3. Last friday, i saw an accident take place.
4. Next sunday is easter sunday.
5. St. patrick's day falls on a thursday this year.
6. Terry and i dressed up as wizards on hallowe'en.
7. They sailed away in january and returned in april.
8. We went shopping on the wednesday before christmas day.

The names of places begin with a capital letter.

(C) Insert the capital letters in the following sentences.

1. The capital city of england is london.
2. All roads in fife were blocked with snow.
3. The football final between derby and oxford will be played in september.
4. We flew into rome on saturday.
5. Paul and maria have an uncle in chicago.
6. She cycled all the way from cardiff to swansea.
7. i received a letter from my pen-pal in spain.
8. Hawick beat kelso by nine points in the final.

The Tall Giraffe

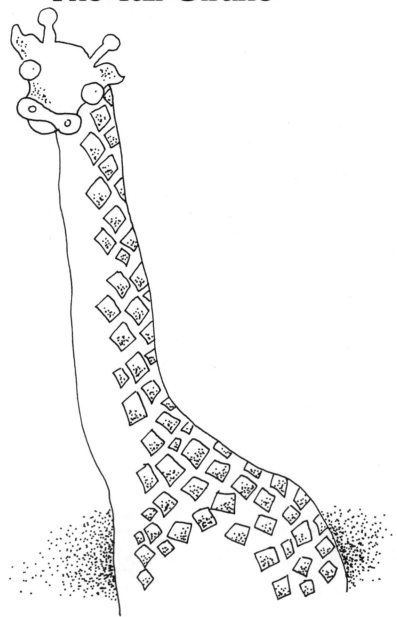

The spotted giraffe is the tallest animal in the world, measuring over 6 metres. He is so tall that a grown man can easily stand upright between his wide front legs. The king of the open brush country lives in Africa.

His shiny grey coat is covered with pretty *patterns*. The small, bony horns on the top of his head are used for "neck fighting" with other giraffes. Did you know that this tall "Skyscraper's" heart is over 60 centimetres long, in order to pump the blood to the top of his head?

It is a *magnificent* sight to see the giraffe plucking the leaves and shoots of the tall acacia tree with his long, black tongue. His thick, hairy lips protect him from prickly thorns and brambles.

The giraffe prefers to sleep standing up so that he can defend himself against attack. A kick from his powerful hind legs can break a man's neck like a matchstick.

The female giraffe gives birth to a single calf. The new-born baby is about 1½ metres tall and at first is *unsteady* walking on his long legs. The mother nurses and cares for her "baby". At the end of the year the young giraffe is strong enough to defend himself. He *roams* with the rest of the herd, across the open *plains* of Africa, just like his forefathers did thousands of years ago.

Look up the words in italics in the dictionary at the back of the book. Write down the meaning of each word.

Questions

1. In what country does the giraffe live?
2. How tall is he?
3. What colour is his coat?
4. What food does he like to eat?
5. How does he defend himself against attack?
6. What use does he make of his bony horns?
7. Why does he sleep standing up?
8. What is a young giraffe called?
9. Why does the giraffe need a large heart?
10. Draw or paint a picture of a giraffe.
    Write 10 interesting sentences about the animal.

The giraffe has a **long** tail.
Which of the following animals have long or short tails?
List: hare, deer, greyhound, pig, squirrel, fox, cow, bear, monkey, kangaroo, rabbit.

Long-tailed animals	Short-tailed animals
....	....
....	....
....	....
....	....
....	....
....	....

Homes

(A) Choose the most suitable word in brackets.

1. A farmer lives in a *(barn, farm house, pen)*.
2. A king lives in a *(hut, castle, cabin)*.
3. A gypsy lives in a *(flat, kennel, caravan)*.
4. A soldier lives in a *(barn, shed, camp)*.
5. A nun lives in a *(church, camp, convent)*.
6. A queen lives in a *(cottage, palace, cave)*.
7. A monk lives in a *(library, monastery, palace)*.
8. A woodcutter lives in a *(college, bank, log cabin)*.
9. A camper lives in a *(office, aeroplane, tent)*.
10. A prisoner lives in a *(cell, tent, mansion)*.

(B) A honeybee lives in a *hive*.

kennel, coop, stable, burrow, web, den, byre, sty, hole, nest.

1. A dog lives in a ....
2. A wild rabbit lives in a ....
3. A spider lives in a ....
4. A wasp lives in a ....
5. A pig lives in a ....
6. A mouse lives in a ....
7. A hen lives in a ....
8. A horse lives in a ....
9. A fox lives in a ....
10. A cow lives in a ....

(C) Write down the correct form of the words in italics.

1. The car is in the *gearga* ....
2. The room in the top storey of the house is called the *ictta* ....
3. A tame rabbit lives in a *chtuh* ....
4. The home in which a snail lives is called a *llesh* ....
5. A small house in the country is a *octtega* ....
6. A house which stands apart on its own is *deacthde* ....
7. Desert people usually live in *settn* ....
8. Stone Age people lived in *scvae* ....

The Animal World

(A) Write a suitable word in the blank spaces below.

Example: Bird is to **nest** as **spider** is to **web**.

1. Pig is to .... as sheep is to lamb.
2. Dog is to .... as hare is to form.
3. Caterpillar is to butterfly as .... is to frog.
4. Kitten is to cat as puppy is to ....
5. Horse is to stable as cow is to ....
6. Paw is to dog as hoof is to ....
7. Shoal is to herring as school is to ....
8. Spider is to fly as cat is to ....
9. .... is to bird as fin is to fish.
10. .... is to goat as nestling is to bird.

(B) Choose the correct word in brackets.

Example: as busy as an *(eel, ape, ant)*
as busy as an **ant**

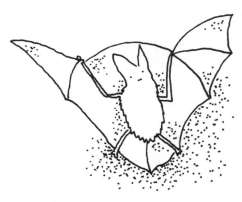

1. as blind as a *(rat, bat, cat)*
2. as graceful as a *(donkey, swan, elephant)*
3. as slow as a *(hare, fox, snail)*
4. as gentle as a *(lamb, hawk, tiger)*
5. as strong as a *(mule, horse, pig)*
6. as swift as a *(robin, hawk, crow)*
7. as hungry as a *(mouse, fox, wolf)*
8. as brave as a *(monkey, deer, lion)*
9. as wise as an *(eagle, owl, ostrich)*
10. as hairy as a *(spider, sheep, gorilla)*

(C) Underline the odd word out in the following lists of words.
Give a reason for your answer.

Example: wren, owl, **bee**, tern, crow. A **bee** is an insect and not a bird.

1. seal, sheep, skunk, sparrow, squirrel.
2. pike, trout, whale, herring, cod.
3. rabbit, badger, otter, fox, hare.
4. peach, pineapple, pear, potato, plum.
5. oyster, mussel, octopus, periwinkle, whelk.
6. fir tree, yew tree, pine tree, beech tree.
7. donkey, kangaroo, mule, jennet.
8. magpie, penguin, cuckoo, robin, blackbird.
9. stallion, filly, colt, buffalo, foal.
10. Husky, St. Bernard, Alsatian, Siamese.

19

A Visit To The Zoo

1A

6A

7D

9D

4A

2D

8D

10A

3D

5A

7.

12D

11D

14A

13A

15A

Lucky Hans

Hans was a country boy. He worked very hard for his master. When he was going home for his summer holidays his master gave him a present of a big lump of gold for his mother.

It was a warm and sunny day. Hans found the gold too heavy to carry. He grew tired and sleepy. Just then a horseman rode along the road.

"You have a fine racehorse," said Hans. "I do wish I had a racehorse instead of this big lump of gold."

The clever horseman saw his chance of a *bargain*.

"I will give you my racehorse for the lump of gold," he said.

The bargain was made and Hans rode away on the fine racehorse. "I am a lucky boy," thought Hans.

It was Hans' first ride on a racehorse without a saddle. The animal *galloped* along the dusty road. The boy had not gone very far when the horse *reared* up and threw him into the air. Hans fell on the road and cut his hands and knees. Just then a farmer passed by with a big, brown cow.

"I wish I had a quiet animal like your cow," said Hans. "Would you like to *exchange* animals?"

The wise farmer knew this was a very good bargain. So, he took the racehorse and gave the cow to the young boy. Hans was very happy.

On and on he walked, driving the cow in front of him. Soon he felt thirsty.

"I will milk the cow," he thought. But when he tried to milk the cow, she kicked him and knocked him on the ground. Luckily, a young butcher boy was driving a fat pig to the market.

"That is a grand pig," said Hans. "I wish I had a pig instead of this silly cow. I would then have some tasty bacon."

The young butcher saw his chance of a bargain.

"I will give you my pig in exchange for your cow," he said.

He took the cow and gave Hans the fat pig.

"I am a lucky boy," thought Hans.

In the next village Hans met a young boy carrying a goose.

"That pig is very like the one that was stolen from our village," said the boy. "If the police catch you, they will put you in jail."

Hans was worried and afraid.

"Oh dear! What shall I do?" he said to the boy.

"I shall take the pig, if you like," said the boy. "You can take my goose."

Hans gladly took the goose. He had not travelled far when he met an old man who was using a special stone to sharpen knives. The man was singing a merry song.

"Why are you so happy?" asked Hans.

"Because I have plenty of money in my pocket," said the old man. "If you had a grindstone like mine, you too could sharpen knives and make plenty of money."

The old man was clever. He knew Hans had no money.

"Give me the goose," he said, "and I will give you a new grindstone."

Hans took the stone and gave the man the fine goose.

"I am a lucky boy," thought Hans.

Soon Hans got tired of carrying the heavy stone. He felt thirsty and stopped for a drink at a stream. As Hans stooped down to drink, the stone slipped from under his arm and sank into a deep pool. Hans did not mind.

"Oh, I am a very lucky young man," he said. "Now I have no load to carry."

Look up the words in italics in the dictionary at the back of the book. Write down the meaning of each word.

Questions

1. What was the name of the story?
2. Who gave Hans a present?
3. What was the present?
4. Where was Hans going?
5. Why did he give away his gold for a racehorse?
6. Do you think it was a good bargain? Tell why.
7. What kind of a cow did Hans get?
8. Why was the boy thirsty?
9. What did the cow do?
10. Why did Hans give away his pig?
11. Where was the young boy going?
12. Whom did Hans meet singing?
13. How did Hans lose the heavy stone?
14. Why did he think he was a lucky boy?
15. Do you think that Hans was a lucky boy? Tell why.

Creative Writing

Sick in Bed

1. **Write a story.**

Helpful words and ideas

.... restless night .... awoke .... felt sick .... bad cough .... throbbing headache .... pain .... my father .... stay in bed .... no appetite .... fever .... rang the doctor .... arrived .... examined .... bottle of medicine .... five days .... much improved ....

A Bad Fall

Helpful words and ideas

.... bored .... orchard .... ripe apples .... nobody around .... climbed .... picked.......... .... lost balance .... fell off .... a sharp, piercing pain .... arm broken .... in agony .... helped home .... brought to hospital .... x-ray .... bad fracture (break) .... arm in a sling .... no sport for a month ....

23

Nature Notes for November

THERE ARE SIGNS ALL AROUND THAT THE YEAR IS COMING TO A CLOSE. THE LEAVES HAVE FALLEN FROM THE TREES AND THE BIRDS HAVE FLOWN SOUTH. THE COUNTRYSIDE GETS READY FOR ITS WINTER SLEEP.

IN THE WOODS, THE LONG-EARED OWL SITS QUIETLY ON A BRANCH. HE IS A NIGHT-TIME CREATURE BUT SOMETIMES HE CAN BE SEEN FLYING NEAR FARM BUILDINGS DURING THE DAY.

THERE IS STILL SOME COLOUR TO BE SEEN. THE LOVELY BRIGHT RED BERRIES OF THE ROWAN TREE BRIGHTEN THE DARK DAYS OF NOVEMBER

POPLAR

NOW THAT THE BRANCHES ARE BARE, IT IS EASIER TO SEE THE DIFFERENT SHAPES OF THE TREES. HOW MANY TREES DO YOU KNOW?

Picture Quiz

1. In which season is November?
2. Which animals go to sleep during winter?
3. Where does the long-eared owl live?
4. What colour are his feathers?
5. Why does he hunt by night?
6. Why has he a sharp beak and claws?
7. What animals does he hunt by night?
8. What fruit grows on the oak tree?
9. Which trees keep their leaves in winter?
10. Name four birds that build their nests in tall trees.
11. Which trees have red berries?
12. What part of the tree is: the trunk? the bark? the fork?
13. Which animal likes to eat hazel nuts?
14. What do we call a place where many trees grow?
15. What do we call a man who makes things from wood?

LARCH

OAK

COMMON ELM

The Full Stop

Always end a sentence with a full stop.

(A) There are three sentences in each of the following. Write them out, putting in the capital letters and full stops.

1. the snow lay deep on the ground it was very cold in the indian **tepee**s although the indians had blankets they were not warm
2. we agreed to meet at the shops when i arrived liam was not there i waited for twenty minutes
3. the robin gave the stick to the squirrel he threw it to the frog the frog took the stick in his mouth and dived into the pond
4. a thick fog covered dublin last night parts of the city were very badly affected motorists were advised to drive carefully
5. a bad storm blew up at sea all the fishing ships made for the harbour the lighthouse-keeper was worried for their safety.
6. sean caught the ball he passed it to terry terry kicked it to shane who slammed it into the back of the net
7. joan lived in a small cottage on the hillside a small stream ran by the house it would dry up in summertime
8. look for a safe place stop and wait look all around and listen before you cross the road

(B) Write out these paragraphs, putting in the capital letters and full stops.

1. one morning peter and his hound went hunting red deer they saw a beautiful lady she was riding towards them on a snow-white horse the lady had long golden hair she wore a robe of silk her horse wore shoes of pure gold peter had never before seen such a beautiful lady
2. william jumped on the white horse behind the princess as the horse galloped away he waved goodbye to peter and his hound soon they reached the edge of the sea it opened before them and they passed through william saw strange fish that no man had ever seen before

The Hidden Treasure

"Wait for me," cried Mary, as her brother Jimmy raced across the field. They were playing "hide and seek" near the old Norman castle

"Hurry up," shouted Jimmy. "We shall be late for tea and Mammy will be angry." Suddenly Mary gave a loud cry.

Jimmy looked behind him and saw his sister lying on the grass. She was crying.

"I tripped over this iron ring and cut my knee," sobbed Mary.

Her left foot was caught in a rusty ring. Jimmy pulled and tugged at the ring. He could not free her leg. Just then Mary got a bright idea. She took off her sandal and slipped her leg out of the iron.

"I wonder why that rusty iron was buried in the ground?" asked Maeve.

"Give me a piece of stick and I shall try to dig around it," said Jimmy.

They found that the ring was fastened to a big iron box. Mary jumped with delight as they hauled the big box up out of the ground. She clapped her hands with joy.

"Maybe there are jewels and gold rings inside the box," she whispered.

"I think it is a pirates' chest with heaps of gold coins," said Jimmy.

He used a big stone to burst open the rusty lock on the box.

"Oh dear!" cried Jimmy as he opened the box. "A pile of old maps and papers. That's all."

"They might be of use to Captain Kelly the owner of the castle," said Mary hopefully. "I think we should show him the maps."

The children ran to the castle gates and rang the door bell. A maid answered the door and told them that Captain Kelly was on a holiday. She thanked the children and took the bundle of maps.

When the children returned home their mother was very angry. The chips and sausages she had fried for the supper were cold. When they told her about their discovery she laughed and said, "I'm afraid you have heard the last about the box and those maps."

The days passed and Mary and Jimmy forgot all about the old treasure chest. Then, one evening Captain Kelly arrived at their house.

"I came to thank you for finding those maps," he said. "One of the maps showed a secret passage that led to a hidden room under the castle. In this secret room I found two boxes of gold coins. Tomorrow I shall show you the coins and the secret tunnel. I have brought along a little present for each of you."

At the garden gate stood two new bicycles. Mary and Jimmy were delighted. They thanked the captain for the lovely presents. Soon they were speeding down the road on their new bicycles.

"Hurry up, slowcoach," shouted Jimmy. "And mind you don't catch your foot in the wheel. Next time you may not be so lucky!".

Questions

1. What was the name of the story?
2. What game were Mary and Jimmy playing?
3. Why were they in a hurry home?
4. What happened to Mary?
5. How did she free her foot?
6. What did Jimmy use to dig around the box?
7. What did she think might be in the box?
8. What did Jimmy think was in it?
9. Why was he disappointed?
10. What did the children do with the maps?
11. Why was their mother angry?
12. Who called to see them?
13. What did he tell them?
14. What presents did he give the children?
15. Why did Jimmy call his sister a 'slowcoach'?

Singular and Plural

Singular means only one.
Plural means more than one.

We say one cat but two cats.
We say one box but two boxes.
We say one church but two churches.

(A) Add *-s* or *-es* to the following words to mean more than one.

1. We say one girl but two ....
2. We say one fox but two ....
3. We say one watch but two ....
4. We say one bush but two ....
5. We say one class but two ....
6. We say one star but two ....
7. We say one witch but two ....
8. We say one thrush but two ....
9. We say one mass but two ....
10. We say one bone but two ....
11. We say one head but two ....
12. We say one wish but two ....
13. We say one box but two ....
14. We say one dish but two ....
15. We say one tree but two ....

16. We say one match but two ....
17. We say one beach but two ....
18. We say one glass but two ....
19. We say one coach but two ....
20. We say one cake but two ....
21. We say one pass but two ....
22. We say one crutch but two ....
23. We say one dash but two ....
24. We say one finch but two ....
25. We say one stone but two ....
26. We say one shirt but two ....
27. We say one stitch but two ....
28. We say one sash but two ....
29. We say one patch but two ....
30. We say one arch but two ....

Words ending in *-AY, EY, OY, -UY* form their plural by adding *-S*.

We say one d*ay* but two day*s*.
We say one k*ey* but two key*s*.
We say one b*oy* but two boy*s*.
We say one g*uy* but two guy*s*.

(B) Complete the following.

1. We say one toy but two ....
2. We say one tray but two ....
3. We say one cowboy but two ....
4. We say one play but two ....
5. We say one turkey but two ....
6. We say one buoy but two ....
7. We say one valley but two ....
8. We say one chimney but two ....

9. We say one donkey but two ....
10. We say one spray but two ....
11. We say one way but two ....
12. We say one jersey but two ....
13. We say one ray but two ....
14. We say one quay but two ....
15. We say one jockey but two ....

Singular and Plural

Nouns meaning one thing are singular.
Nouns meaning more than one thing are plural.

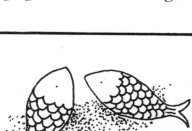

Examples: We say one dog but two dogs.
We say one mouse but two mice.

Words ending in -F **usually** form their plural by changing -F to -V and adding -ES

Example: We say one **thief** but two **thieves**.

(A) Write the plural of the words in bold type.

1. The **hunter** shot the **wolf**.
2. The **butcher** bought the **calf**.
3. The **supporter** wore the **scarf**.
4. The **insect** fed on the **leaf**.
5. We ate the **fish** and the **loaf** of bread.
6. The **shoemaker** gave the **present** to the **elf**.
7. **He** cut the **rope** with the **knife**.
8. The **carpenter** repaired the **shelf**.

(B) Fill in the singular or plural form of the word in the table below.

Singular	Plural	Singular	Plural
foot	....	....	potatoes
....	children	baby	....
lady	....	....	sheep
....	salmon	army	....
man	....	....	toes
....	pennies	trousers	....
piano	....	....	women
....	cod	tooth	....
safe	....	....	duties
....	geese	scissors	....
hero	....	....	echoes
....	deer	cry	....
party	....	....	grasses
....	flies	....	volcanoes

The Moon

Some Facts

1. Many people believe that the moon was once part of the earth and broke away millions of years ago. Other people say that it came, not from the earth, but from another part of space.

2. There are high mountains, deep *valleys* and wide flat spaces on the moon. At one time, huge rocks crashed into the moon making large holes which are called craters. These craters can be many *kilometres* wide and some of them have walls which are two kilometres high.

3. Animals and plants cannot live on the moon because it has no air and no water. There are no clouds, no rain and no snow.

4. Sound needs air to travel. Because there is no air on the moon, there can be no sound there. The moon is a silent place.

5. The moon has no light of its own. It looks bright because the sun's light shines on it.

6. One day on the moon lasts for two weeks. During the day, the rocks become hotter than boiling water. This is because the moon is closer to the sun than the earth. One night on the moon also lasts for two weeks. It becomes so cold that a person would freeze to death within minutes.

7. The moon is 238 thousand miles away from earth. It takes a spaceship only three days to reach the moon. But it would take a car almost six months to travel this distance.

8. It takes the moon 27 days, 7 hours, 43 minutes and 12 seconds to travel around the earth. As it passes over the earth it is able to pull the waters of the earth upwards. It is this pull which causes the tides to flow and ebb.

Look up the words in italics in the dictionary at the back of the book. Write down the meaning of each word.

Questions

1. How far is the moon away from the earth?
2. Why can there be no life on the moon?
3. What is a crater?
4. Why can there be no sound on the moon?
5. Why is the moon hotter than the earth?
6. How long does a night on the moon last?
7. What causes the tides to flow and ebb?
8. Which day of the week is named after the moon?
9. Do you think people will be able to live on the moon one day?. Give a reason for your answer.
10. Write down anything else you know about the moon.

A Walk On The Moon

On the 20th July, 1969, people all over the world sat and watched their television sets. Two men from earth had landed on the moon. Years of hard work, and a lot of money, had been spent in trying to put a person there. Now, these two men were about to step out and take the first walk on its *surface*. They knew that their spacesuits would save them from the great heat outside the spaceship. They had put their air tanks on their backs so that they could breathe when they walked out onto the moon. When they were ready, they slowly opened the door of their small spaceship. Neil Armstrong stepped out and started to climb down the short ladder. As he put his left foot down on the moon, he said: "That's one small step for man — one giant leap for *mankind*." At the age of thirty eight, Neil Armstrong had become the first person to set foot on the moon.

At last, they began to walk. The two spacemen noticed that the moon was covered in dust, which stuck to their boots. Here and there, small rocks were to be found. At first, it was not easy to walk on the moon. If you weigh sixty kilograms on earth, you will weigh only ten kilograms on the moon. So the two men had to be careful that they did not trip and fall. Soon, however, they got used to being so light and began to hop, skip and jump about. But they only had enough air to give them three hours on the moon. There were rocks to collect and tests to be done. When they were finished, they left a message on the dusty ground. It said: "Here, men from planet earth set foot upon the moon, July 1969. We came in peace for all mankind."

Look up the words in italics in the dictionary at the back of the book. Write down the meaning of each word.

Questions

1. Why were people watching T.V. on the 20th July, 1969?
2. Why did the men wear spacesuits?
3. What did they carry on their backs?
4. Who stepped out first?
5. What did he say when he put his foot down on the moon?
6. Why was it not easy to walk on the moon?
8. Why did they not stay longer?
9. What was the message they left there?
10. Why do you think the spacemen wanted to bring rocks back to earth?

Creative Writing

The Hungry Fox

Write a story about the night a fox came to steal a farmer's chickens.

Helpful words and ideas

.... moonlit night .... silent hills .... prowling fox .... lonely
farmhouse .... sneaked around .... small outhouse .... sleeping hens
.... slunk towards .... crept under .... snatched .... hens
.... great commotion (noise and panic) .... scurried (ran quickly) ....
fled .... farmer awoke .... stairs .... shotgun .... searched
.... no trace ....

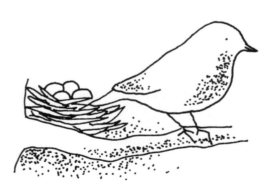

The Robin's Nest

Write a story about discovering a robin's nest near your home.

Helpful words and ideas

.... springtime .... bright sunshine .... birds singing .... noticed
a robin .... perched on .... flew quickly into .... followed .... an
old kettle .... a small, neat nest lined with .... five tiny eggs .... tiptoed
away .... two weeks later .... returned five, fluffy chicks .... cheeping
and chirping .... hungry .... busy parents .... worms .... visited
each day until ....

Nature Notes For December

THIS IS THE TIME OF YEAR FOR MISTLETOE AND HOLLY. WE ALL LOVE THE RED BERRIES OF THE HOLLY TREE BUT THE BEAUTIFUL SHINY HOLLY LEAVES HAVE SHARP PRICKLES. THE LEAVES AT THE TOP OF THE TREE HAVE NO PRICKLES. I WONDER WHY?

MISTLETOE GROWS ON THE BRANCHES OF OTHER TREES. BIRDS EAT THE JUICY BERRIES OF THE MISTLETOE AND THE SEEDS STICK TO THEIR BEAKS. THE BIRDS CLEAN THEIR BEAKS ON NEARBY BRANCHES AND THE SEEDS FALL INTO CRACKS IN THE WOOD. THESE SEEDS GROW INTO MISTLETOE LATER.

DON'T FORGET TO LEAVE FOOD AND WATER FOR THE BIRDS. THE GROUND IS OFTEN TOO HARD FOR THEM TO GET FOOD AND WATER FOR THEMSELVES.

Nature Quiz

1. Why do birds like the mistletoe?
2. How do birds plant the seeds of the mistletoe?
3. What kind of leaves grow on the holly tree?
4. When do we decorate our homes with sprigs of holly?
5. Which trees keep their leaves all the year round?
6. Why do some trees have prickles?
7. What is made from the timber of fir trees?
8. What fruit grows on fir trees?
9. What is a man called who works in a forest?
10. Where do we usually see the robin?
11. Where does he like to build his nest?
12. What does he like to eat?
13. What is the father robin called?
14. Why does the robin dislike the snow and ice?
15. How did the robin get a red breast?

OUR 'CHRISTMAS TREES' ARE REALLY SPRUCE FIRS. THESE TREES CAME FROM NORWAY ABOUT FOUR HUNDRED YEARS AGO.

How To Address An Envelope

This is how the name and address should be written on an envelope.

Miss Anne Robson,
106 Valley Road,
Duffield,
Derbyshire, DE1 3PY.

(i) The name of the person is put on the first line. When writing to a woman, we put Mrs., Miss or Ms. before the name. When writing to a man, we use Mr.

(ii) The number of the house and road name are written on the second line.

(iii) On the third line is placed the name of the town, village or local area.

(iv) The county and the postcode is placed on the fourth line.

(A) Write your name and address on an envelope like this.

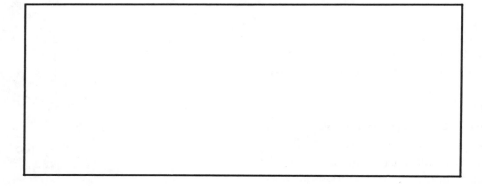

(B) Draw envelopes and address them to the following people:

1. Your best friend.
2. The Principal, at the school address.
3. Your uncle or aunt.
4. Mr. John Whelan, 24 Larkin Road, Exeter, Devon EX7 1AB.
5. Ms. Joan Dougan, 18 Brandon Drive, Dalkeith, Midlothian EH6 3PB.

Robin Redbreast

Cock robin, with his gay red breast, brown wings and *plump* body, is a tame and popular bird. He hops about our gardens and lawns, picking up worms, insects and caterpillars. While we are digging in the garden the little robin likes to sit on the edge of the wheelbarrow. He keeps a sharp look out for juicy snails and wriggling worms. He will even *perch* on the handle of the spade and entertain us with his sweet chirping.

Each cock robin lives in one or more gardens and his space is called his **territory**. It is his home and he is unwilling to share it with other robins. He sings sweetly and loudly during the summer and winter to show that he is in *occupation*. His song tells the other robins to keep out of his *territory*. Robin redbreast seldom sings outside his own territory.

If the cock robin finds another robin *trespassing* on his territory he will draw himself up, fluff out his breast feathers to make himself appear as large as possible and sing at the top of his voice. He will then stand in front of the invader and sway from side to side so that his red breast is clearly *visible*. The invader usually retreats back over the border but if he remains he is attacked and driven out.

If a hen robin turns up, at first she is chased away, but after some time she is accepted by the cock and allowed to live in a part of the territory, provided she keeps out of his way.

During the breeding season, in March or early April, the cock and hen robin become friends and go about together. They build a nest in some bush, *shrub*, or shed. The hen robin does most of the building while her partner entertains her with his loud singing. She uses twigs, leaves and bits of paper to fashion the nest. Cock robin will feed the hen as she needs extra food to produce the eggs. She lays 3-7 whitish eggs which take about 13 days to hatch.

When one of the fledglings is ready to be born it pecks on the shell wall with its special egg-tooth. The shell cracks and a small hole appears. When the hole is large enough the young robin sticks out its head. It struggles until the shell breaks and it is free. If there are any difficulties, the mother will come to the rescue of her young.

When the fledglings hatch they are naked and it takes them a couple of weeks to grow feathers. Both parents feed the young with soft earthworms, baby caterpillars and small snails. They teach them how to fly and find food. The young robins are speckled and do not develop the red breast until autumn. In less than 3 weeks the young birds are strong enough to fly away and find new territories for themselves. In July most robins shed their old feathers and grow new ones. Did you know that the hen robin may have as many as 3 broods in a breeding season?

Many young robins die in the first year. Cats, rats, and owls kill some of them but the cold weather is their worst enemy. The snow and ice make it difficult for them to find insects, worms and berries. The poor birds depend on the food they can find outside our kitchen doors and the crumbs we give them. Do not forget to feed our feathered friend, the robin, during the cold and frosty weather.

Look up the words in italics in the dictionary at the back of the book. Write down the meaning of each word.

(A) Questions Answer the questions in sentence-form where possible.

1. Where do we usually find the robin?
2. How is it shown that he is a friendly bird?
3. What food does he eat?
4. What is a robin's territory?
5. How does the cock robin chase away an invader?
6. When is the breeding season?
7. What colour are the robin's eggs?
8. Describe the young robins.
9. Why do so many young robins die?
10. How can we help the robins in winter?
11. A robin **chirps**.
    What bird: (a) hoots (b) coos (c) screeches (d) screams (e) caws (f) quacks.
12. A robin feeds on insects and snails.
    What do the following creatures feed on: (a) hawk (b) spider (c) fox (d) rabbit (e) rat (f) otter (g) hedgehog (h) shark.
13. Here is a verse of poetry written by a 10 year old pupil.
    > "Robin, Robin, Redbreast,
    > Skimming through the trees,
    > Bringing home the food,
    > To feed its hungry brood."

    Now try and write a poem about the robin.

36

Capital Letters (revision)

Remember

Capital letters are used for:-

(i)   The beginning of a sentence. **My** sister is sick.

(ii) The names of people, titles of people. Is **D**octor **S**mith at home?

(iii) The names of places. She travelled to **N**ew **Y**ork.

(A) Insert the capital letters where necessary in the following sentences.

1. the seagull built her nest high up on the cliff.
2. my pet dog has a sore paw.
3. an otter lives in a holt.
4. peter and james are brothers.
5. her best friend is elizabeth brown.
6. marion and helen went walking in the park.
7. catherine is taller than richard.
8. the plane flew from shannon to london.
9. mother teresa lives in calcutta.
10. captain cook sailed around the coast of australia.

Capital letters are used for:-

(i)   "I" when used on its own. When she arrived **I** left.

(ii) The names of week-days and months. **M**onday comes before **T**uesday.

(iii) The names of special days and festivals. **D**ecember 25th is **C**hristmas **D**ay.

(B) Insert the capital letters where necessary in the following sentences.

1. i fed the calves in the farmyard.
2. i am certain i was the first to see the eagle.
3. she and i collected sea shells.
4. schools are closed during july and august.
5. sunday is a church holiday.
6. march 17th is saint patrick's day.
7. on easter sunday the lord rose from the dead.
8. the teacher told a story about palm sunday.
9. children attend school from monday to friday.
10. the three months of winter are november, december and january.

> 30 days have September,
> April, June and November
> All the rest have 31,
> Except February alone,
> Which has but 28 days clear,
> And 29 in each leap year.

The Little Match Girl

It was Christmas Eve and snow lay deep on the ground. Night was falling and it was very, very cold.

A little girl stood at the corner of a city street. Her clothes were in rags and her shoes were torn. She held out small boxes of matches to the crowds of people passing by, but nobody bought any matches. She stood at the corner of the street all day, without a penny in her pocket.

The little match girl grew colder and colder. In the evening she took shelter from the falling snow. She lit a match to keep herself warm.

The match burned brightly and, looking at it, the little girl saw a big room and a bright fire. When the flame went out, the big room disappeared. Nothing was left but the cold and the darkness.

The little girl lit another match. She saw again the same room. This time a crowd of happy children were sitting around a dinner table. On the table was a big, fat goose, but when the match flame went out, the room *vanished*. It was cold and dark once again.

The girl lit a third match. This time she saw a lovely Christmas tree with lights. When the match burned out, the lights rose into the sky and the match girl saw that they were stars.

One of the stars fell, and the child remembered that her dead grandmother had often told her that every time a star falls, a soul goes to heaven.

As she lit another match, the girl saw her dear old grandmother. She kept on lighting match after match *lest* her grandmother would disappear like the goose, the tree and the room.

"Do not go away, Granny," *pleaded* the match girl. "Stay with me or take me with you."

Her grandmother did not leave her. She reached down and took the little girl in her arms. They rose high into the sky and disappeared through the golden gates of heaven.

There would be no more cold or hunger for the little match girl. She was with God.

In the morning an old man found her little body in the doorway of a house, with all the burnt out matches beside her. The police said that she had been trying to warm herself.

The people wondered why she had a beautiful smile on her face. They did not know of the lovely things she had seen or of the great joy that filled her heart when her grandmother took her up to heaven with her.

Look up the words in italics in the dictionary at the back of the book. Write down the meaning of each word.

Questions

1. What was the name of the story?
2. Which season was it?
3. Who was standing at the street corner?
4. How was she dressed?
5. What was she selling?
6. How many boxes of matches did she sell?
7. Where did she shelter from the snow?
8. Why did she light a match?
9. What did she see when she lit the second match?
10. What fell from the sky?
11. Who came to visit the little match girl?
12. Where did her grandmother take her?
13. Who found the body of the little girl?
14. Why, do you think, the little child had a smile on her face?
15. Make up a new name for the story.

Nature Notes For January

ALTHOUGH MOST GROWING THINGS TAKE A HOLIDAY DURING THE COLD WINTER MONTHS, THERE ARE A FEW BRAVE LITTLE PLANTS TO BE SEEN.
SHEPHERD'S PURSE IS STILL BLOOMING. YOU CAN FIND IT GROWING ON WASTE LAND IN A NICE SHELTERED SPOT.

WHEN THE WEATHER IS STORMY, GULLS FLY INLAND TO LOOK FOR FOOD.

IF SNOW FALLS, LOOK OUT FOR TRACKS OF ANIMALS

THE LITTLE FIELD-MOUSE TRAILS HIS LONG TAIL BEHIND HIM, LEAVING A LINE BETWEEN HIS FOOTPRINTS.

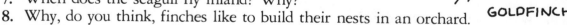

IF YOU SEE WHAT LOOKS LIKE PAIRS OF EXCLAMATION MARKS, MR. RABBIT HAS PASSED THIS WAY.

A FOX LEAVES A TRACK OF SINGLE FOOT-PRINTS. THIS IS BECAUSE HE PUTS HIS HIND FEET INTO THE TRACKS OF HIS FORE-FEET

THE DULL JANUARY COUNTRYSIDE IS BRIGHTENED BY THE LOVELY COLOURS OF THE FINCH FAMILY.

CHAFFINCH

GOLDFINCH

Nature Quiz

1. In which season is January?
2. Which plant blooms in January?
3. What colour is a seagull?
4. Where does he build his nest?
5. Why has the seagull webbed feet?
6. What food does he like to eat?
7. When does the seagull fly inland? Why?
8. Why, do you think, finches like to build their nests in an orchard.
9. Why have finches strong beaks?
10. How would you know a bullfinch?
11. Why is it cruel to keep a goldfinch in a cage?
12. Name four garden birds.
13. Where is the best place to look for animal tracks? Say why.
14. What kind of tracks does a fox make?

BULLFINCH

Masculine and Feminine

The word **"king"** is a masculine word because it refers to a male person.
The word **"queen"** is a feminine word because it refers to a female person.

(A) Write the following words in their correct boxes. An example is given.

List: prince, nephew, aunt, waitress, uncle, niece, waiter, actor, actress, princess.

Masculine:	boy					
Feminine:	girl					

(B) Write the feminine form of the words in bold type. *(Study page 92)*.

1. The **waiter** served the **duke**.
2. The **ram** frightened the **boy**.
3. The **bridegroom** had no **brother**.
4. The **manager** hired a new **waiter**.
5. The **lord** spoke to the **priest**.
6. The **leopard** killed the **colt**.
7. The **abbot** met the **prophet**.
8. The **gander** and the **drake** swam in the pond.
9. The **fox** attacked the **cock**.
10. The **stallion** chased away the **lion**.

(C) Write the masculine form of the words in bold type *(Study page 92)*.

1. The **landlady** spoke to her **daughter**.
2. The **queen** argued with the **witch**.
3. The **bride** listened to **her mother**.
4. The **poetess** praised the **goddess**.
5. His **granddaughter** became a **nun**.
6. The **widow** met **her sister** at the airport.
7. The **heroine** of the story was a young **headmistress**.
8. The **mayoress** paid the **tailoress**.

The Lobster

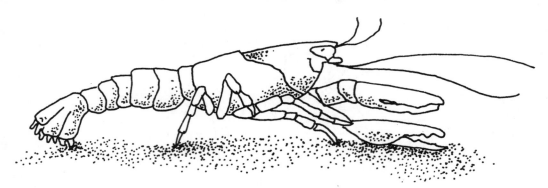

Lobsters have lived in the sea for millions of years. These shellfish crawl around the ocean floor on slender legs. They are protected by their strong shells.

The lobster lives in *shallow* waters around our coasts. Just like the fish, he breathes through tiny blood vessels in his gills. His long feelers help him find food among the rocks and seaweed. At night he hunts for dead fish, shellfish, snails and water insects. The hungry lobster will even devour his brother or sister. If he loses a claw or a leg, he grows a new one. What a strange creature!

The female lobster cleverly glues her eggs to the underside of her body. She carries them with her until they are hatched. Many of the baby lobsters are eaten by the bigger fish. Those that escape, hide among the rocks or bury themselves deep in the sand. There they grow big and strong. Each summer they are fitted with a new suit of *armour* and a fresh stomach lining. They hide in some dark hole until the new crusty shell hardens.

Fishermen catch lobsters in *funnel-shaped* pots. A piece of fish is used as *bait*. Once a lobster crawls into a pot, he is trapped.

Lobster is one of the world's favourite seafoods.

Look up the words in italics in the dictionary at the back of the book. Write down the meaning of each word.

Questions

1. Where does the lobster live?
2. How many legs has he?
3. How does he protect himself?
4. What food does he eat?
5. Where does the female lobster carry her eggs?
6. How does the lobster breathe?
7. What dangers await the baby lobsters?
8. How do fishermen trap lobsters?
9. What do you think is strange about the lobster?

Questions

Always start a question with a capital letter and end it with a question mark.

Who won the race?
Where does she live?
What age is Paul?

(A) Write out these questions correctly, putting in the capital letters and question marks.

1. in what class are you
2. who is the captain of the school team
3. when are you going to the circus
4. which pencil is yours
5. where shall we go after school
6. can you lend me your ruler
7. whose hat is this
8. what did the teacher say
9. are you going to the seaside tomorrow
10. why did she not come
11. how many pupils are there in your class
12. do you go to bed early
13. where is the new teacher
14. who broke the window
15. whose dog is in the school hall

(B) Write questions for which the following sentences are the answers.

1. She is eight years of age.   (*What* .... ?)
2. School starts at nine o'clock.   (*When* .... ?)
3. It is his book.   (*Whose* ....?)
4. The inspector came to the school.   (*Who* .... ?)
5. She cried because she was sick.   (*Why* .... ?)
6. The pigeon perched on the roof.   (*Where* .... ?)
7. The front wheel of the car fell off. (*Which* .... ?)
8. They live four kilometres from Oxford. (*How* .... ?)
9. The train arrived at noon.   (*When* .... ?)
10. Money is kept in a bank.   (*Where* .... ?)

A Great Day

Jill and her best friend, Sue, were watching a show on the television. There was a competition on — and they were going to enter. The prize for the winner was a free trip to London ànd a visit to the BBC. They listened carefully as the lady called out four questions:

"How many days are there in a leap year?
What is a fox's tail called?
Who cut off the tails of the three blind mice?
How many teeth does a person have in a full set?"

Both girls felt sure that they knew the four answers. They wrote their answers on a card and went out to post it. Ten days later, this short letter came back from the BBC.

BBC,
Ealing,
London.
19/7/88

Dear Jill and Sue,

I am pleased to tell you that you have won the competition on our show. We would like you to come on the show next Friday. I am sending you free tickets for the train to London. I will meet you at the station and look after you for the day.

Yours truly,
Joan Power.

The two girls were delighted with their news. They could not wait for Friday to come. All week long, they made plans for their trip to London. When the big day came, they rose early and went to catch the train. They were in London by ten o'clock that morning. Joan Power was there to meet them.

"Where would you like to go in London?" she asked with a smile.
"To the zoo," said Jill.
"To Oxford Street," said Sue.

The lucky girls were brought to both places. First, they went to the zoo. Sue had been there once before, but it was Jill's first visit. She stared at the giraffes, laughed at the monkeys and screamed when she saw the snakes. Jill had the time of her life. Next, Joan Power drove them to Oxford Street, as part of their prize, they had been given ten pounds each. Now they went to spend it in the big shops. Jill and Sue bought presents for everyone at home. Then it was time to go to the BBC for the television show.

Back at home, the families and friends of the two girls were sitting and watching their t.v. sets. At half past four, the show started. Everyone waited for Jill and Sue to appear.

"We have two clever girls on our show this week," said Joan Power, at last. "They are the winners of our competition - Jill Hope and Sue Warn."

Everybody in the studio at the BBC clapped. Everybody at home cheered. It was a moment the two girls would never forget.

Questions

1. What was the prize for the competition?
2. What did the letter tell the girls?
3. Who met them at the station in London?
4. Where did they go first?
5. Why did Jill want to go there?
6. What did they do in Oxford Street?
7. What began at half past four?
8. What do the letters BBC mean?
9. Write about your favourite T.V. show.
10. Could you have answered the four questions in the competition.

How To Write A Letter

Read this letter that Tom wrote to his uncle in Wales.

---

(1) 23 Riverside Avenue,
Dorset,
Sheffield, S10 5HT.
(2) 10th September, 1988.

(3) Dear Uncle Cliff,

(4) Many thanks for the lovely present of the watch you gave me for my birthday. I have always wanted to own a watch and I am so happy now that I have one. It keeps very good time. My mammy tells me that from now on I will have no excuse for being late for school.

I hope that you are well and that Bran is taking good care of the sheep for you. Once again, many thanks for the beautiful watch.

(5) Yours sincerely,
(6) Tom

Note:

1. The writer's full **address** is at the top right-hand side of the page.
2. The **date** should be placed a little below the address. The above date could also be written as 10/9/1988 or 10/9/88 or September 10th, 1988.
3. The **greeting** is written on the left-hand side of the page. Note the use of the capital letters and commas.
4. Start a new paragraph for the **message** of the letter.
5. There are different ways of **ending** a letter. Examples: Yours faithfully, Yours truly, Yours respectfully, Your good friend, With best wishes.

6. The writer's **name** should be clearly written beneath the ending. Note the use of the full stop.

Exercises

1. Write a short letter to a friend who is sick in hospital.
2. You are spending a week in your cousin's house beside the River Severn. Write a letter to someone at home.
3. Write a letter to a famous person asking for his/her autograph.
4. Write the letter which you think that famous person might send back to you.
5. Write a letter to a pen-pal in another country.

Submarines

The submarine works in a simple way. All submarines have large tanks which can be filled with water or air to make the ship submerge or rise. When the tank is filled with water, the submarine becomes so heavy that it will sink. To stop the submarine from sinking all the way to the bottom of the sea, some water is pumped back out of the tanks. This will keep the submarine at the same depth. In order to come up again, the tanks are emptied of water and filled with air. The submarine is now light enough to rise to the surface.

The first submarine was built in 1803 by an American named Robert Fulton. It could only carry two people and its *propeller* had to be worked by hand. Yet Fulton knew that his machine could be of great use to any army at war. At that time, England and France were at war in Europe. So he travelled to France where he tried to sell his new invention to Napoleon. Even though he *succeeded* in blowing up a target ship with his submarine, the French were not interested. They thought it a most unfair way to fight a war. The *crafty* American then went to England, hoping to sell his submarine there. Two raids were made against French ships, but did not succeed. No one, at that time, was interested in Fulton's invention.

Today, of course, huge submarines travel through the waters of the world. Some of these ships are more than 200 metres in length, can move at a speed of 45 knots (55 miles per hour) and can dive to great depths. In 1958, a U.S. submarine sailed under the ice to the North Pole. And in 1960, another U.S. ship sailed around the world without once raising to the surface.

Look up the words in italics in the dictionary at the back of the book. Write down the meaning of each word.

Questions

1. How does a submarine rise?
2. How does a submarine sink?
3. What did Robert Fulton do in 1803?
4. Why did he travel to France?
5. Why were the French not interested in his invention?
6. How fast can today's submarines travel?
7. Where did a submarine sail to in 1958?
8. Can you name three of the world's oceans?
9. Try to make as many words as you can from s - u - b - m - a - r - i - n - e.
10. Pretend you are a sailor on board a submarine. Write a paragraph about life on board your ship.

Nature Notes For February

FEBRUARY IS CALLED 'FILL-DYKE', BECAUSE IT IS USUALLY A VERY RAINY MONTH. NATURE IS BEGINNING TO STIR AGAIN AND THERE ARE SIGNS THAT WINTER WILL SOON BE OVER AND SPRING IS ON ITS WAY.

MRS. SONG-THRUSH IS ONE OF THE FIRST BIRDS TO BUILD A NEST. WHILE HER HUSBAND SITS ON A NEARBY BRANCH SINGING MERRILY, SHE WEAVES A LOVELY NEST OF GRASS, ROOTS AND TWIGS.

SNOWDROPS HANG THEIR HEADS TO PROTECT THEMSELVES FROM THE COLD WIND.

THE PRETTY CROCUS CAN ALSO BE SEEN ABOUT THIS TIME.

YELLOW CATKINS MAKE THE HEDGES LOOK BRIGHT AND CHEERFUL.

Picture Quiz

1. Why is February called "fill dyke"?
2. Which are the months of spring?
3. What are the signs of spring?
4. What is your favourite flower in spring?
5. Where would you look for snowdrops?
6. Why do they hang their heads?
7. What colour is the snowdrop? the crocus?
8. What do yellow catkins remind you of?
9. Where does the song-thrush build her nest?
10. What does she use to build it?
11. What colour is the song-thrush?
12. What are young foxes called?
13. Where are young foxes born?
14. What is the mother fox called?
15. Why is the fox's tail called a "brush"?

THE FOX IS LOOKING FOR A RABBIT HOLE THAT HE CAN TAKE OVER. IT WILL BE A HOME FOR HIS VIXEN AND THE CUBS WHICH WILL BE BORN IN MARCH OR APRIL.

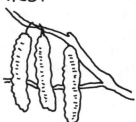

Nouns

A noun is the name of any person, place, animal or thing.

Examples   **Susan** is the name of a person.
                Derby is the name of a place.
                Dog is the name of an animal.
                Pencil is the name of a thing.

(A) Write the nouns which are the answers to the following.

1. A person who sells meat ....
2. A place where money is kept ....
3. An animal which builds dams ....
4. A thing used for looking at stars ....
5. A person who flies aircraft ....
6. A place where hay is stored ....
7. An animal that spins a web ....
8. A thing which is used for digging ....

(B) Pick out the nouns in these sentences.

1. The small cat swam across the wide river.
2. A young child was playing happily in the garden.
3. He gathered nuts and wild strawberries in the woods.
4. Two horses pulled the cart along the street.
5. The wise man sat in the chair and told a long story.
6. We went to York to visit our aunt.
7. The children saw the man catch the thief.
8. The monkey escaped from his cage in the zoo.
9. The angry girl shouted loudly at the barking dog.
10. The old man walked slowly along the dusty road.

(C) Write three nouns for each of the following groups. The first one is done for you.

1. Fish:	trout	shark	mackerel
2. Dogs:			
3. Countries:			
4. Vegetables:			
5. Cities:			
6. Toys:			
7. Insects:			
8. Fruit:			
9. Flowers:			
10. Sports:			
11. Farm Animals:			

Elton, The Golden Eagle

Elton is a handsome golden eagle. He lives in the wild and lonely Scottish Highlands. This giant "king of the air" has a wingspan of more than two metres. He is proud of his magnificent dark-brown *plumage*, with its golden *tints*. He has a hooked bill and strong, sharp *talons* which help him snatch his prey.

His keen eyesight makes him an excellent hunter. He feeds on rabbits, hares, birds, squirrels, *carcasses* of dead animals and even new-born lambs. He is able to spot a running rabbit at a distance of over 3 kms. If you or I had the eagle's sharp eyesight, we could read the print on a newspaper a half kilometre away! Now you know what a person means when he says, "you have the eye of an eagle". When Elton spies his prey, he descends out of the sky at a speed of over 200 kilometres per hour. His victim has little chance of escaping. In a single graceful movement he snatches it with his powerful talons. He returns to his nest and circles it a few times before zooming in to land. He folds his magnificent wings, and from his high nest he *scans* the surrounding countryside.

Elton's nest is built on a rocky cliff ledge. It is called an eyrie. It is made from sticks, leaves and clumps of heather. The inside of the nest is lined with grasses, ferns and feathers. Year after year the same nest is used by the couple. Rotting bits of food and bird droppings are strewn about the foul-smelling nest. One eyrie, discovered in America, had over two tonnes of sticks and was over six metres deep.

The female eagle lays 1-3 large eggs. In most nests only one eaglet hatches out. If another one is born, the two eaglets fight and only the strongest survives. The new-born eaglet is weak and flops around the nest. The parents feed the baby with tasty *morsels* of food. When the eaglet's wings are strong enough, it makes its first solo flight, watched by the proud parents. Every day it practises flying, in preparation for the day when it will leave home and live on its own. It takes an eagle 4 or 5 years to grow the rich golden plumage of an adult bird.

Do you think that the golden eagle is worthy of the title "king and ruler of the sky?"

Look up the words in italics in the dictionary at the back of the book. Write down the meaning of each word.

Questions

1. Where does Elton live?
2. What colour is he?
3. How does he snatch his prey?
4. What food does he eat?
5. How do you know the eagle has sharp eyesight?
6. Where does he built his nest?
7. What is an eagle's nest called?
8. How long does it take an eagle to grow adult golden feathers?
9. How did the wren become king of the birds?
10. The eagle is a bird of prey.
    Name these birds of prey.
    (1) F............ (2) H............ (3) V............
    (4) B............ (5) K............
11. The eagle's nest is situated on a high mountain or cliff. Name two birds which nest:
    (a) in trees (b) by the sea (c) on the ground (d) in barns or sheds (e) on or near river banks.

How To Write A Postcard

Read carefully this postcard which Maria has written to her uncle.

---

(2) Kintyre
(3) 10/7/88

(4) I am having a great time here in Kintyre. The weather is fine and I have been swimming each day. Tom and I cycled out into the hills today. We are going on the boat to the Aran Islands tomorrow. Daddy and Mummy send their love. Wish you were here.

(1) Mr. John Murphy,
   27 Seaview Road,
   Corby,
     Northants, N10 5XT.

(5) Best wishes,
(6) Maria.

Notice these six points on the card:

1. The **name** and full **address** are given. When writing to a man, Mr. is used. When writing to a woman, Mrs., Miss, or Ms. can be used.
2. The name of the **place** from where the card is sent should be written at the top.
3. The day, the month and the year are shown in the **date**.
   (10/7/88 means the tenth day of the seventh month of the year 1988).
4. The **message**.
5. Notice the use of the capital letter and the comma in the **ending** of the card.
6. The **signature**: a full stop is placed after the sender's name.

Exercise

1. Pretend you are on holidays in Spain. Write a postcard to a member of your family who has stayed at home.
2. Write a postcard to a pen-pal in the United States or Canada telling him or her about Britain.
3. Think of a place you would like to visit. Write a postcard to your best friend telling about it.
4. Choose one of the above three cards and draw the picture for that postcard.

Farmyard Animals

7D

2D

3A

11D

1A

6A

8D

3D

9D

8A

5A

11A

12D

4D

14A

10A

15A

13D

Confusing Words

"Two" "To" "Too"

Examples:
(i)   The **two** swallows built their nest in the barn.
(ii) The doctor came **to** see me.
(iii) My sister is **too** young to go to school.

Fill in the blank spaces in the following sentences with either "to", "two" or "too".

1. They have .... television sets in their house.
2. The .... boys cycled .... the seaside.
3. It is .... early .... go .... bed.
4. Early .... bed and early .... rise, makes one healthy, wealthy and wise.

5. The child was .... excited .... sleep.
6. I am going .... the pictures with my .... friends.
7. The .... lambs loved .... play with their mother.
8. The teacher spoke .... the .... boys in the last row.
9. There were .... many people trying .... get into the hall.
10. It is not easy .... refuse a favour .... a friend.
11. The problem was .... difficult .... solve.

"It's" or "Its"

(i)   IT's .... means .... 'it is'.
(ii) ITS .... means .... 'belonging to it', and is followed by a noun.

Examples:
(i)   The swift returned to **its** nest.
(ii) **It's** a beautiful day.

Fill in the blank spaces in the following sentences with either "its" or "it's".

1. .... raining outside.
2. The hedgehog's spines protect it from .... enemies.
3. The car rolled over on .... side.
4. .... going to be a fine day.
5. The cuckoo left .... egg in the other bird's nest.
6. My pet cat hurt .... front paw.
7. The meat has lost .... flavour.
8. .... a long way to Tipperary.
9. The ostrich is proud of .... feathers.
10. .... better late than never.
11. The bull tossed .... head in the air.
12. The friendly dog wagged .... tail and opened .... mouth.

The Cart Race

When Terry heard about the cart race, he ran to call on his best friend, Tim.

"I've just heard some great news, Tim," "There is going to be a big cart race in the park next Saturday. Would you like to enter?"

"I would," said Tom. "But there is one small problem. We have no cart."

"I can fix that," answered his friend. "We will make one today."

The two boys knew where to go to make their cart. They went to "Barney's place," down by the canal. Barney was a kind, friendly old man who lived in a small white house near the canal bridge. He had a scrap-yard at the back of the house where they would find just what they needed. Barney was sure to help.

"Go around the back and see what you can find," said Barney when they called.

Terry and Tim rushed into the scrap-yard. It was full of scrap — old cars, bits of wood, broken prams and all kinds of odds and ends. They had come to the right place. In no time at all, they had found wood and wheels for the cart. A few minutes later, Barney came out the back door with a box of tools.

"Now, let's get to work on this racing car," was all he said.

By five o'clock that evening, the job was done. The old man and the two boys took the cart outside to see how it would work. It moved like the wind. All during the week at school, they kept it a secret. Each day after school, they worked on the cart in Terry's garage. First they cleaned it. Then they painted it bright red and yellow. Tim's lucky number was eight, so they put a big number 8 on the sides of the cart. In black paint at the back they put the letters T and T. Now they were ready for the big race.

A huge crowd turned up at the park on the Saturday. Twelve carts had entered for the race. Many fathers and mothers, brothers and sisters, as well as friends were there. Barney had come along to watch too. Everybody was wondering who would win the big silver cup.

All the carts were lined up at the top of the hill. "Five— — — —four— — — —three — — — —two— — — —one— — — —" and away they went! There was a loud cheer as the carts began to roll down. Number 8 got off to a good start. Terry sat in front, with Tim behind. Terry was doing the steering, Tim was working the brakes. Coming to the third bend, they were in third place. Suddenly, a cart hit them from behind and they were in trouble. Tim had to pull hard on the brakes to stop them from crashing. Two carts passed them out as they slowed down. They were now in fifth place, coming to the last bend. There was only one hundred and fifty metres to go. It was then that Number 8 began to move.

"Come on! Number 8!" shouted Barney from the crowd.

First, one cart and then another and another was left behind. With only twenty metres to the finish, they flew past the leader. The crowd cheered wildly. Barney threw his cap up into the air. Terry and Tim had won the cup.

Questions

1. Why did Terry call on his friend?
2. Where did Barney live?
3. Why did they call on Barney?
4. What did they do each day after school?
5. What do you think the letters T and T stood for?
6. How many carts were entered for the race?
7. What was the first prize?
8. What happened at the third bend?
9. When did Number 8 begin to move?
10. Why did Barney throw his cap into the air?

The Pygmy Shrew

It is difficult to spot a pygmy shrew. It is so small a creature, less than 5 centimetres long, that it can easily hide in the *meadows* and hedgerows. If you listen carefully you may hear its high-pitched squeak as it *scampers* through the long grass. It is brownish-grey in colour and has a pointed *snout* and a long tail, just like a field mouse.

The hungry shrew feeds on what it can find — beetles, snails, butterflies, slugs and crickets. It sniffs out its prey and with lightning speed, leaps upon it. Within seconds it gobbles up an insect or a small animal. This tiny animal eats its own weight in food every 3 hours. It would die in a day if left without food. It is able to kill a rat with its razor-sharp teeth. If it can find no other food, the starving shrew will *devour* one of its brothers or sisters.

The female shrew makes a nest of leaves and grasses. The new-born babies are no bigger than honey-bees. They are so tiny that 2 of them could fit on a teaspoon. They are fed on a diet of small worms and juicy snails. In a few weeks the young shrews are strong enough to leave the nest and live on their own.

This small animal has a special gland in its body that gives off an unpleasant smell. This smell protects it from its enemies — foxes, badgers and birds of prey.

Look up the words in italics in the dictionary at the back of the book. Write down the meaning of each word.

Questions

1. Where would you find the pygmy shrew?
2. Describe what it looks like?
3. On what does it feed?
4. How does it catch its prey?
5. How much food would a pygmy shrew eat in 6 hours?
6. When do the young leave the nest?
7. Write two ways in which the pygmy shrew can defend or protect itself.
8. Complete the following:

   (a) as busy as an a — —
   (b) as sly as a f — —
   (c) as gentle as a l — — —
   (d) as fierce as a l — — —
   (e) as slippery as an e — —
   (f) as hungry as a w — — —

Creative Writing

An Adventure In Space

1. Pretend you are a spaceman who has landed on another planet. Write a story about your adventure.

Helpful words and ideas

.... spaceship .... a large planet .... landed safely .... opened .... stepped out .... looked around .... walked slowly .... huge rocks .... strange planets .... explored .... towards a hill .... climbed .... looked down .... deep, green valley .... shock and surprise .... a huge, red dome (round building) .... higher than .... wider than .... to get a closer look .... crept towards .... hid behind .... suddenly I saw ....
Continue the story.

The Old House

2. Pretend that you are staying with your cousins down the country. Your cousins want to show you an old house which they say is haunted. But you don't believe in ghosts. Write a story about what happened.

Helpful words and ideas

.... set out together .... across the fields .... a fine, sunny day .... laughing .... joking .... through the woods .... came to a pathway .... a rusty old gate .... creaked loudly .... overgrown garden .... tall, dark building .... broken windows .... open door .... entered .... as quiet as mice .... hall .... dust on the .... cobwebs on the .... big stairs .... stepped softly .... then we heard ....
Continue the story.

Nature Notes For March

SPRING IS HERE AT LAST. NEW BUDS CAN BE SEEN ON HEDGES AND TREES. LAMBS JUMP AND PLAY IN THE MEADOWS.

THE BLACKTHORN IS IN FULL BLOSSOM. LEAVES DO NOT APPEAR UNTIL LATER.

BY THE SIDE OF THE STREAM, MARSH MARIGOLDS MAKE A SPLASH OF COLOUR.

MARCH IS A BUSY MONTH FOR THE BIRDS. NESTS ARE BUILT AND EGGS ARE LAID

HERE ARE SOME OF THE EGGS TO BE SEEN.

BLACKBIRD   SONG THRUSH   HEDGE SPARROW   ROBIN

YOU MUST NEVER REMOVE EGGS FROM A BIRD'S NEST.

FROGS AND TOADS LAY THEIR EGGS. SNAILS WAKE UP FROM THEIR WINTER SLEEP.

Nature Quiz

1. When are new-born lambs seen in the fields?
2. What sound do they make?
3. What is the name given to a man who looks after sheep?
4. What wild animal often kills new-born lambs?
5. What covering has a sheep?
6. What clothes are made from wool?
7. What colour flowers grow on the blackthorn tree?
8. How would you know a blackthorn tree?
9. Where would you find marsh marigolds growing?
10. Why is the March hare a funny fellow?
11. Where does the hare live?
12. Why has the hare very long ears?
13. What colour is a grown bullfrog?
14. Where does the snail live?
15. Why should you never touch a bird's nest?

THE MARCH HARE IS A FUNNY FELLOW. HE LEAPS AND PRANCES AND 'BOXES' HIS RIVALS.

The Cuckoo

In early spring, the welcome cuckoo returns from Africa to the land of its birth. The cuckoo is a beautiful bird. It has a blue-grey back, white-tipped tail, pointed wings and is pale-grey underneath with dark stripes.

The cuckoo does not build a nest, so the lazy hen cuckoo lays her eggs in other birds' nests. She chooses a nest with eggs, eats one of them and lays her own egg in its place. The clever cuckoo *selects* a nest with eggs that are like her own in colour, shape and size.

When the young cuckoo hatches out, it throws the rest of the eggs and nestlings out of the nest. The foster-parents feed the young cuckoo as if it were their own. Soon the cuckoo grows big and strong on a *diet* of fat caterpillars, juicy worms and hairy spiders.

Did you know that the hen cuckoo may lay as many as fifteen eggs? She lays her eggs in such nests as the wagtail's, hedge-sparrow's and the meadow-pipit's. The male cuckoo sings his well-known call as he flies from place to place.

At the end of summer, the young cuckoos fly away to warmer lands. Their first *adventurous* journey is made without any help from their parents. Indeed, the old birds *migrate* long before the young ones.

Look up the words in italics in the dictionary at the back of the book. Write down the meaning of each word.

Questions

1. Describe the cuckoo.
2. Why can the cuckoo be called a 'lazy' bird?
3. What does the young cuckoo do when it hatches out?
4. How many eggs might a cuckoo lay?
5. In which nests are these eggs laid?
6. How do you think the cuckoo gets its name?
7. Africa is one of the continents of the world. Can you name the other four continents?
8. What have the following creatures got in common: owl, badger, moth, bat, fox?

Choosing Interesting Words

It is important to choose the correct word that best expresses our meaning. A little practice is necessary.

Example: The old tramp went up the hill.
The word **"went"** does not express the meaning we want to convey. It would be much better to say:-
(i)   The old tramp **staggered** up the hill.
(ii) The old tramp **limped** up the hill.
(iii) The old tramp **stumbled** up the hill.

Instead of the word "went", insert one of the words in the given list below.

1. The train **went** through the station.
2. The swallow **went** into the barn.
3. The fox **went** into the chicken coop.
4. The worm **went** along the ground.
5. The horse **went** across the field.
6. The duck **went** across the road.
7. The pony **went** smartly around the race track.
8. The monkey **went** from branch to branch.
9. The dog **went** out the door.
10. The soldier **went** up the road.
11. The rabbit **went** into its burrow.
12. The brave man **went** into the river to rescue the little girl.
13. The slimy snake **went** across the grass.
14. The man **went** into the bank.

List of words: flew, marched, dived, cantered, crawled, sneaked, wriggled, thundered, swung, ran, waddled, trotted, walked, scurried.

Instead of the word "ate", insert one of the words in the given list below.

1. The lion **ate** the young deer.
2. The python **ate** the wild pig.
3. The cow **ate** the green grass.
4. The mouse **ate** the cheddar cheese.
5. The turkey **ate** the mashed potatoes.
6. The hen **ate** the oats in the pan.
7. The small girl **ate** a lollipop.
8. The tall boy **ate** a red apple.

List of words: licked, nibbled, devoured, pecked, gobbled up, chewed, swallowed, munched.

Fairy Candles

Many years ago there lived in Scotland a great *chieftain* called the White Captain. One day, one of his servants came to him looking for help.

"The fairies have stolen my wife," said the man. "They have taken her to the Hill of the Ants. I have visited the hill and heard music and dancing inside. I heard my wife singing and laughing."

"I think I can help you," said the White Captain. "Go to Black John who lives across the hill from here. Tell him I sent you and ask him for one of his fairy candles. The fairies have given him these magic candles which allow him into the places where they hold their meetings."

The servant went to Black John's house. Black John gladly gave him a fairy candle for the White Captain.

"The fairies will try and steal this candle from you," said Black John. "Whatever you do, don't look behind you on your way home."

As the man rode back to the White Captain, he heard the sound of a galloping horse behind him. He was about to turn around when he suddenly remembered what Black John had told him, and he rode on.

Next, he heard the sound of *carriage* wheels and cries of, "Catch him! Catch him!" A funny laugh made him look behind. Suddenly, the fairy candle was no longer in his hand.

He returned to Black John for a second candle. John gave him the candle and also a big, black stone.

"When you come to the river, throw this stone across and see what happens," said Black John. "The fairies do not like the water."

Once again the fairies followed the man. But this time he never looked back. When he came to the river he threw the black stone across the water. *Immediately* he was lifted into the air and landed on the other bank. The fairies were very angry but they did not follow him across the river. Soon the servant reached the home of the White Captain.

Next day, the servant and the White Captain, who carried the candle, went to the Hill of the Ants. The moment they lit the fairy candle, a door appeared in the side of the hill. The two men went inside. They saw the man's wife dancing a reel with the King of the Fairies.

The fairies were very angry when they saw the two men. They flew around them like buzzing bees. But the fairy candle *protected* the White Captain and his servant. The man rescued his wife from the King of the Fairies. Just as the three of them stepped outside the fairy hill, the great door closed behind them.

The man's wife was surprised to hear that she had been away for a year and a day.

"I thought I had only been there for one night," she said. "The fairies were very kind to me and I enjoyed their parties."

Look up the words in italics in the dictionary at the back of the book. Write down the meaning of each word.

Questions

1. What was the name of the story?
2. What was the chieftain's name?
3. Why did the servant come to him for help?
4. What was the name of the fairy palace?
5. What sounds did the man hear coming from the fairy hill?
6. Who had the fairy candle?
7. What warning did John give the servant?
8. How did the man lose the first candle he got?
9. What did Black John give the man the second time?
10. What did he tell him to do with the stone?
11. Why did the fairies not cross the river?
12. What happened when the White Captain lit the candle?
13. What did the two men see inside the fairy palace?
14. Why did the fairies not capture them?
15. How long was the man's wife inside the fairy hill?

Descriptive Words

The **little white** kitten played with a **fluffy** ball.

The words "little", "white" and "fluffy" are descriptive words or adjectives. They tell us more about the kitten and the ball.

Study the different adjectives used below to describe the hen.

a **frightened** hen	a **hungry** hen	a **white** hen	an **angry** hen
a **little** hen	a **fat** hen	a **cackling** hen	an **old** hen

(A) Pick out the adjectives in the following sentences.

1. The big dog killed the brown rat.
2. The pretty butterfly landed on the red rose.
3. The grey squirrel cracked a hazel nut.
4. The gentle white lamb played in the green field.
5. The rich man bought a fat pig.
6. The timid mouse ate the fresh cheese.
7. The grizzly bear lived in the deep woods.
8. The sly fox killed a plump duck.
9. The horrid beetle crawled under a mossy stone.
10. The small black horse drank the clear water.

(B) Write an interesting adjective to describe each word below. Put each new adjective and matching word in a sentence.

cat	apple	bird	clown	ring

Reynard, The Fox

Reynard, the red fox, is one of our best known wild animals. He is easily recognised by his reddish coat. The tip of his long bushy tail is white. The fox's ears, like those of a gun dog, are always pricked to enable him to catch sounds of danger. His large eyes shine in the dark just like a cat's.

Reynard lives in our woodlands and forests. More and more he is visiting our town parks and raiding our dustbins in the early hours of the morning. This *cunning* animal has special "smelling posts" scattered throughout his territory. They warn other foxes and animals to keep out. At night, foxes talk to one another by barking.

During the summer months the dog fox lives in a den — a hollowed out hole in the ground. The fox usually has several of these dens in his territory. In winter he lives with the female fox, called a **vixen**, in an underground home or **earth**. It is often an *enlarged* burrow or some badger's *abandoned* home. In this earth the young cubs are born. The vixen cares for her blind and helpless cubs while the dog fox hunts for food to feed his family. Throughout the summer months the vixen teaches the young foxes how to trap and *stalk* animals. Sometimes the parents hide food in order to develop the young foxes' sense of smell. At the end of the summer, they leave the "earth" to live and hunt on their own.

Reynard hunts alone at night. His *keen* sense of smell and sharp hearing make him an excellent hunter. He likes to eat rats, rabbits, mice, chickens, birds and wild fruit. When he scents a fieldmouse in the long grass he pounces on the little creature and pins it to the ground. It is then easy for him to catch the mouse in his strong jaws and kill it. The wily fox is able to trap and kill other animals by imitating their sounds. He can bleat like a lamb and squeal like a rabbit. The fox is also one of the few animals that is able to unroll a spiny hedgehog and eat it.

Some foxes have strange ways of getting rid of fleas. One clever fox was seen to wade into deep water with a long stick gripped between his teeth. The fleas crowded onto the fox's head. As the fox ducked lower and lower in the water the fleas made a mad scramble down his nose and onto the stick. The happy fox released his *cargo* of fleas and smiled as it floated away in the current.

The red fox is the farmer's enemy. At daybreak he sneaks into the chicken coop and snatches a fat duck or a plump chicken. Silently, the fox hurries into the nearby woods with his victim slung across his back.

The fox also loves to play hide-and-seek with the hounds. He is such a master trickster that he seems to enjoy leading them astray. He throws the dogs off the scent by doubling back on his tracks and running across a swift-flowing stream. In the end the panting dogs and tired hunters give up the chase. The *gallant* fox returns to his den to live and fight another day.

Look up the words in italics in the dictionary in the back of the book. Write down the meaning of each word.

(A) Questions: Answer the questions in sentence-form where possible.

1. What kind of a tail has a fox?
2. Where are the cubs born?
3. What name is given to a female fox?
4. Where do the parents live in the winter?
5. What lessons are taught to the cubs?
6. How does the fox trap the field mouse?
7. What clever way has he of getting rid of fleas?
8. Why does the farmer dislike the fox?
9. How does Reynard escape from the hounds?
10. Draw or paint a picture of a fox.
    Write 10 interesting sentences about the animal.

The Right Word In The Right Place

(A) Choose a suitable "colour" word from the given list to fill in the blank spaces.

Example: The long, green grass waved in the summer breeze.

List: black, yellow, brown, evergreen, grey, golden, hazel, red, white, blue, tawny, purple, dark-skinned, fair-haired, pink, silver-grey, green-eyed, sky-blue, piebald, speckled.

1. The gardener sprayed the .... roses.
2. The .... leaves withered and died.
3. The .... trout leaped out of the water.
4. The elephant has .... ivory tusks.
5. The .... daffodils swayed in the evening breeze.
6. The .... beetle laid her eggs under a mossy stone.
7. The hills were covered with .... heather.
8. The .... firs were covered with snow.
9. The Vikings were .... warriors.
10. The .... owl hooted in the woods.
11. The small squirrel cracked the .... nuts.
12. The .... natives swarmed around the boat.
13. A .... mist hung over the valley.
14. The lark sang in the clear .... sky.
15. The .... stallion roamed the prairies.
16. The .... monster rose out of the sea.
17. The hedge-sparrow's nest had four .... eggs in it.
18. An Indian rode into the fort on a .... pony.
19. The salmon's flesh is a pale .... colour.
20. The .... ears of corn waved gently in the breeze.

(B) Fill in the blank spaces with a suitable word from the given list.

Example: She spoke softly to the child.

List: bravely, sweetly, briskly, loudly, easily, slowly, carefully, heavily, angrily.

1. The soldier fought .... but in the end he had to surrender.
2. The boat moved .... against the strong tide.
3. Walk .... when out late at night.
4. Colette sang .... at the school concert.
5. The policeman knocked .... on the door.
6. The old woman fell .... on the slippery road.
7. John was .... the best student in the class.
8. The farmer spoke .... to the boys.
9. The postman walked .... up the footpath.

Nature Notes For April

WILD FLOWERS ARE STARTING TO APPEAR EVERYWHERE AND TREES LIKE THE ELM, OAK, LARCH AND SYCAMORE ARE ALL IN BUD.
BIRDS ARE BUSY BUILDING NESTS AND REARING THEIR NEWLY BORN FAMILIES.

PRIMROSE

WOOD VIOLET

WOOD-SORREL

BIRD'S EYE SPEEDWELL

LESSER CELANDINE

WOOD ANEMONE

COWSLIP

BLUEBELL

BIRDS AND BUTTERFLIES BEGIN TO ARRIVE BACK AFTER A HOLIDAY IN THE SUNNY SOUTH

SAND MARTINS RETURN TO THEIR OLD HOMES — TUNNELS DUG IN SANDY CLIFFS

SWALLOWS CAN COME FROM SOUTH AFRICA AND FLY STRAIGHT TO THEIR OLD NESTS, WHICH THEY LEFT AT THE END OF THE PREVIOUS SUMMER.

Nature's Quiz

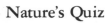

1. Why are birds busy in April?
2. What is a baby bird called?
3. Why should you never touch birds' eggs?
4. What birds are kept as pets?
5. Name two birds that cannot fly.
6. Where do swallows fly to during the winter?
7. What material does a swallow use to build her nest?
8. What food does she like to eat?
9. Name another bird that comes to Britain in April or May.
10. How did these birds get their names: sand-martin, wagtail, swift, kingfisher?
11. What name is given to a group of birds flying together?
12. Which trees begin to bud in April?
13. Which flower do you like best?
14. What insects visit flowers? Why?
15. Why do people water flowers at the end of a warm day?

The First Lighthouse

Two thousand, three hundred years ago, work began on the world's first lighthouse. The order to build it came from the King of Egypt, who wanted it to be the first, the biggest, and the best lighthouse the world would ever see. Thousands of workers were brought to the small island off Egypt's coast, where the building was to be placed. It was to be many years before their work was done. First, they had to lay down a large square building on which to put the lighthouse tower. When the tower was completed, it stood over 150 metres high. It had eight sides and was built of white *marble*. At the top of this great tower was the lantern of the lighthouse. And on top of the lantern was placed a huge bronze statue of the sun-god. What a sight it must have been!

By day and by night, a bright fire was kept burning in the round lantern of the lighthouse. Wood for the fire was carried to the top by means of a lift which went up through the centre of the tower. It was a lift worked by water power — another invention of the clever Egyptians. But the most brilliant idea of all was the way they used a big mirror to *reflect* the light from the fire out across the sea. It was said that the light could be seen for forty five kilometres. During the day, the great white building was a fine landmark for any sailors at sea. During the night, the powerful *beam* of light helped to guide ships and to warn them of the rocks along the coast.

Egypt's lighthouse became known all over the *ancient* world and was listed as one of the Seven Wonders of the World. It stood for almost fifteen hundred years until it was finally destroyed by an earthquake. Sadly, there is hardly a trace left of this building today.

Look up the words in italics in the dictionary at the back of the book. Write down the meaning of each word.

Questions

1. Where was the lighthouse built?
2. Who ordered it to be built?
3. What was placed on top of the lantern?
4. How was wood for the fire brought to the top?
5. What was the mirror used for?
6. Why do you think the lighthouse was built of white stone?
7. For how long did the building last?
8. What is the purpose of a lighthouse?
9. Pretend you are the world's first lighthouse-keeper in Egypt. Write a paragraph about your job.
10. Try to find out more about the Seven Wonders of the World.

Action Words

Verbs are 'action' words. A verb is a word which tells us that a person, place or thing does something or is something. Examples The boy **walked**.

London **is** our capital city.

The apple **will fall**.

The dog **was barking**.

(A) Pick out the verbs in these sentences.

1. The children posted the letters.
2. The bus will leave at seven o'clock.
3. The puppy is eating the meat.
4. They slept in a shed near the river.
5. Maria was reading a book in the library.
6. The phone rang in the hall.
7. A small bird flew into the bush.
8. Owls usually come out at night.
9. David will cook the dinner on Friday.
10. The police stopped the car outside the town.

(B) Choose a verb to fill the blank spaces below.

1. The dog .... Joe on the leg.
2. Mary .... a big fish in the pond.
3. Hundreds of people .... the parade.
4. A bear .... smaller than an elephant.
5. The nurse .... in the hospital.
6. His train .... tomorrow morning.
7. Anna .... a great goal.
8. We .... them outside the church.
9. Everybody .... loudly when they heard the news.
10. The fox .... across the river.

(C) Complete each sentence using a suitable verb.

1. The brave girl ....
2. A kind old man ....
3. Two strong horses ....
4. A huge army ....
5. The clever boy ....
6. The ugly duckling ....
7. A mean thief ....
8. The rusty old car ....
9. The rugby team ....
10. Her jealous sister ....

The Shy Kingfisher

The brightly-coloured kingfisher is called a **"flying jewel"**. It wears a robe of brilliant blue, green and orange colours. It lives near our rivers, streams and lakes. The kingfisher's nest is built at the end of a long narrow tunnel, dug under a sandy bank or stream. The passageway can be up to two metres long. The nest is made from fish bones. During the breeding season the female lays between 2-8 *glossy* white eggs, which hatch after three weeks.

Both parents take care of the *nestlings*. They feed them on a diet of fish, insects and small eels. At the first sign of danger the young kingfishers run backwards up the sloping tunnel. When they are strong enough, they are chased out of the nest by their parents. Now they begin to fish for themselves and *occupy* a new stretch of the river bank. Birds of prey, like the hawk, seldom attack kingfishers because they dislike their foul-smelling flesh.

The kingfisher is an excellent fisherman. It perches on a low branch overhanging the water and waits patiently for its prey to come along. As soon as it spots a fish, it *plunges* its red dagger-shaped bill into it. The speared fish is lifted out of the water and swallowed. Later on when the parents are feeding their young, they regurgitate (throw out) the *digested* fish.

The shy kingfisher may have as many as three broods in a breeding season.

Look up the words in italics in the dictionary at the back of the book. Write down the meaning of each word.

Questions

1. Why is the kingfisher called a 'flying jewel'?
2. Where does it build its nest?
3. How long does it take the eggs to hatch?
4. What do the nestlings eat?
5. Why are kingfishers rarely attacked by hawks?
6. How do the parents feed their young?
7. List five other birds which you would find on a river in Britain.
8. Write each of these words in an interesting sentence: hopped, glided, swooped, darted, hovered.

Sam, The Stone Age Man

Imagine you are living in the Stone Age. We are going to visit Sam, the Stone Age Man. He and his family are dressed in animal skins. They live in a cold damp cave not far from the banks of the River Lagan. Sam chose his site because of the need for a *regular* supply of fish and fresh water. Sometimes he kills a wild boar or deer that comes to drink at the water's edge. Sam's family lives on a diet of fish, wild fruit and a *variety* of berries.

Sam uses sharp flint stones, from the nearby hills, to make weapons. By grinding and hammering the pieces of flint, he fashions strong arrowheads, axes and other tools. Animal *sinews* and strips of leather are used to tie the razor-sharp flints to the tips of wooden handles. With these stone weapons, he hunts and kills wild boars, bears and wolves. Even today, tribes like the Dani of New Guinea, the bushmen of the Kalahari Desert and the Aborigines of Australia make stone tools.

Sam often goes on hunting trips with his friends. He is one of the most skilful hunters and trackers in the *region*. He has tamed two wild dogs for hunting. A hunting trip with Sam is always an exciting event. It usually takes the hunters a few days to track down and kill the giant Irish elk. When this great animal is trapped it fights for its life. Only a hunter of Sam's skill and courage can kill it.

There is always great *rejoicing* and shouting when the hunters return home carrying the giant elk. That night there is a feast. The women carve up the animal with their sharp stone knives. The meat is roasted on a spit over a blazing fire. Everybody sits around the fire, chewing the delicious meat and listening to Sam tell about the great hunt. When supper is over, the womenfolk tidy up the camp site while the men plan their next hunting trip.

Next day, the women clean and scrape the hides with sharp flint scrapers. The skins are softened by chewing them for hours and rubbing them with oil. The women stitch the hides together, using bone needles and animal sinews as thread. The animal's teeth are *fashioned* into pretty necklaces and bracelets.

Children who lived in the Stone Age led exciting lives. The wild forest was their playground. There, they learned the secrets and wonders of nature.

Look up the words in italics in the dictionary at the back of the book. Write down the meaning of each word.

Questions

1. Where did Sam and his family live?
2. What wild animals roamed the forests?
3. Why did Sam choose to live near a river?
4. What food did his family eat?
5. What weapons had Sam?
6. How did he make them?
7. What tribes still make stone tools?
8. Why did Sam tame the wild dogs?
9. How was the giant elk roasted?
10. How did the women soften the hides of the animals?
11. What sewing materials had the women?
12. What use was made of the animal's teeth?
13. What secrets, do you think, did Stone Age children learn in the deep forests?

14. Give another title for this story.
15. Stone Age man lived in a **cave**. Where do the following people live?
    (a) A gypsy lives in a c ....
    (b) A prisoner lives in a c ....
    (c) A lumberjack lives in a log c ....
    (d) A prince lives in a c ....
    (e) A Swiss skier may live in a ch ....
    (f) A nun lives in a c ....
    (g) A soldier lives in a c ....
    (h) A family on holiday in the country may live in a c ....

The Dog — Man's Faithful Friend

Scientists tell us that the dog has been living on this earth for millions of years. We know that Stone Age man tamed wild dogs. His cave paintings show hunting scenes of dogs. Indeed, many skeletons of dogs have been discovered in Stone Age caves.

Nobody knows exactly how man first tamed the dog. Perhaps he bred wild dogs from wolves, which he had trapped. Later his tamed dogs were trained to protect his cattle from wild animals.

The first tamed dogs may have looked like an Australian wild dog, called a dingo. These dogs hunt in packs and kill sheep and lambs. They are a great danger to the flocks of the Australian sheep-farmers.

The Fly

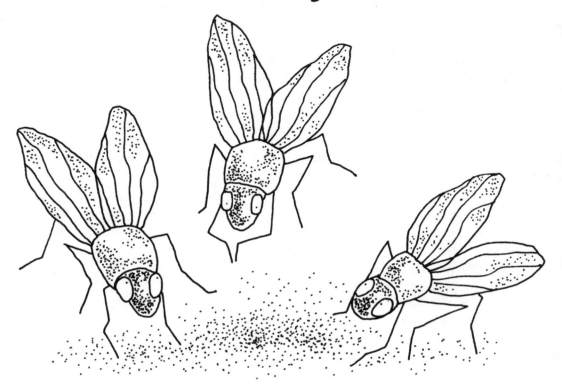

The common housefly, that buzzes around the kitchen, is a pest, a killer and a disease carrier. Her dull grey body is covered with short, *stubby* hairs. She has five eyes — two large purple-brown ones and three smaller ones. Just like a periscope on a submarine, she can turn her thin neck in all directions. Did you know that her six hairy legs have a pair of claws at the end of each one? She uses these claws for trapping her enemies. Behind her two beautiful *transparent* wings are two knobs which give her balance. Near her eyes are two short, feathery feelers or antennae. These are used to feel and smell food and to sense approaching danger.

The female fly breeds and multiplies quickly. Every ten days she lays 100-150 white eggs. These eggs are laid on some rubbish dump, manure heap or rotting food. Within a day, the legless white maggots wriggle out of the eggs. They feed on the garbage around them. They shed their outer skins a few times before rolling themselves into oval-shaped cocoons. In less than 10 days they emerge from the cocoons, full-grown flies. They are now ready to spread their germs everywhere. Thanks to the spiders, frogs, lizards, rats and wasps for devouring millions of these dangerous insects.

The fly is not choosey about what she eats. Her tiny mouth is like a drinking straw sucking up soft and juicy food. The horrible fly uses *droplets* of dirty liquid from her own body to soften hard food. Now you know the reason for all those dirty fly specks on windows and walls.

The amazing housefly beats her wings 200-300 times a second. Yet, she can remain *aloft* for hours. On the underside of each foot the fly has two soft *suction* pads that *secrete* a sticky substance. This is the reason why she is able to walk up a smooth wall or across a ceiling.

The average housefly lives 30-40 days during the hot summer months. In cooler weather she may live for more than four months. Millions of them die during the cold and bitter winter. However, enough survive to make sure the species is not wiped out.

If we are to win the fight against the hateful fly we must not leave food *exposed*, dustbins uncovered, or rotting food lying around.

Look up the words in italics in the dictionary at the back of the book. Write down the meaning of each word.

(A) Questions

1. Why is the fly dangerous?
2. How does she see in all directions?
3. What helps her to keep her balance?
4. What use does she make of her feelers?
5. Where does she lay her eggs?
6. When do they hatch?
7. What creatures feed on flies?
8. How does the fly soften her food?
9. How is she able to walk upside-down across a ceiling?
10. What can we do to keep the fly population under control?
11. Name one disease transmitted by flies?
12. Draw a colourful poster for a campaign against flies.

(B) Flies fly

Name two creatures which:- (i) crawl (ii) swim (iii) waddle (iv) climb

(C) Story

Pretend you are a fly: Tell how you narrowly escaped from a spider.

Helpful words and phrases

fine close-meshed web .... spider waiting and watching .... frame of strong threads .... you alighted at the edge of the web .... sticky .... frantic efforts .... panic .... escape.

Nature Notes For May

May is the month of the flowers. Our old friends, the buttercups and daisies are enjoying the sunshine and the air is sweet with the perfume of the hawthorn, (sometimes called 'the May blossom').

In ponds all over the country, mother frogs have laid their eggs. Tiny tadpoles come out of the eggs and some time later, become frogs.

The bees are busy, gathering pollen from the flowers. These are worker bees. The lazy drones sit around doing nothing!

The eggs are covered with a thick jelly.

Tadpoles eat the plants in the water.

After eight weeks, hind legs appear.

Two weeks later the front legs grow.

12 weeks after hatching, the tail drops off and the tadpole becomes a frog.

Nature Quiz

1. Name four wild flowers which bloom in May.
2. Why does the honeybee visit the flowers?
3. Where does the honeybee live?
4. What work does she do in the hive?
5. How does the bee protect herself?
6. What sound does the honeybee make?
7. What is a drone?
8. Where does the frog live?
9. What does he like to eat?
10. What is a young frog called?
11. How does the grown frog trap flies and insects?
12. What sound does the frog make at night?
13. Where would you see the stoat?
14. What other animal is very like the stoat?
15. Name two other animals that love to jump in the air?

Did you ever see a stoat dancing?

Stoats love to jump and twist around and do backward somersaults!

Arion And The Dolphin

Arion was the best singer and poet in Greece. He became so famous that the king asked him to come and live in the royal palace. Every morning, he played on his harp and sang to the nobles of the court.

One day the king sent for Arion.

"You will have to go to a music festival in Italy," he said. "I am sure you will win the competition. The first prize is a bag of gold coins."

"I do not want any gold," said Arion, "but I would like to win the *competition*."

"You will travel in one of my royal ships," said the king. "But you must return to my palace after the competition."

Arion promised to return to the king. He sailed across the sea to Italy. The best musicians in the world were at the festival. When Arion's turn came, he sang so sweetly and played so well on his harp, that the judges gave him first prize. Arion was given a huge bag of gold coins. The people begged him to remain in Italy but Arion remembered his promise to the king. He went down to the harbour and *boarded* the king's ship. He stood on the *deck* and waved goodbye to his many friends.

During the night the cruel captain and his crew made up their minds to kill Arion and take his gold. Arion was taken prisoner and brought before the wicked captain.

"You are too rich," roared the captain. "You must die."

"*Spare* my life and I will give you the gold coins," begged Arion.

"You might change your mind when we reach Greece," said the captain. "It would be dangerous to let you live."

"Please *grant* me a last wish," pleaded Arion. "Let me sing another song and play my harp before I die."

"You may do that," agreed the captain.

While Arion sang his song and played on the harp a school of leaping dolphins swam around the ship, dancing to his sweet music. When the song was over, Arion leaped into the sea. At once an old dolphin swam underneath him. Arion climbed on his back, and the happy dolphin swam back to Greece.

The king was happy to see Arion but became very angry when he heard that the ship's crew had robbed him and tried to kill him. As soon as the ship arrived in the harbour the king sent for the captain and his crew.

"Where is my musician Arion?" he asked.

"The young boy would not return with us," said the wicked captain. "He stayed in Italy with his friends."

At that moment, Arion stepped into the room. When the captain and the sailors saw him, they were frightened.

"It is a ghost!" cried the captain. "Arion is dead. I saw him jump into the sea."

The angry king punished the captain and his crew. They were thrown into prison.

Arion stayed in the king's palace and became the most famous musician in Greece.

Look up the words in italics in the dictionary at the back of the book. Write down the meaning of each word.

Questions

1. What was the name of the story?
2. Who was Arion?
3. What musical instrument did he play?
4. Why did he go to Italy?
5. What was the first prize?
6. How did he travel to Italy?
7. Why did the judges give Arion first prize?
8. Why did Arion not remain in Italy?
9. Who robbed him on the way home?
10. Why was the captain afraid to let him live?
11. What was Arion's last wish?
12. What happened when he played his harp for the last time?
13. How did the dolphin help Arion?
14. What excuse did the captain give the king?
15. How did the king punish the cruel captain and his crew?

Verbs

The **verb** is in the singular when we speak of **one**.
The **verb** is in the plural when we speak of **more than one**.

Examples:
The man **is** sick. The men **are** sick.
The girl **was** pretty. The girls **were** pretty.

(A) Fill in the blank spaces with either "is" or "are".

1. Jane and I ...... going on a nature walk.
2. The tigress ...... angry because her cubs ...... lost.
3. You ...... fond of animals but she ...... not.
4. The racehorse ...... injured and her hooves ...... bleeding.
5. When the cat ..... alseep the mice ...... awake.
6. The frog ...... in the damp grass and the tadpoles ...... in the marshy pond.
7. Tony and Peter ...... going bird-watching when the evenings ...... brighter.
8. We ...... going to visit the zoo in the afternoon.
9. The honeybees ...... buzzing and the pigeon ...... cooing.
10. It ...... a fine day and we ...... motoring to the seaside.
11. Miss Lucy ...... our teacher and we ...... her pupils.
12. Margaret ...... frightened because there ...... spiders in her room.

(B) Fill in the blank spaces with either "was" or "were".

1. There .... a wasp in the classroom and the girls .... nervous.
2. The sow .... killed and her litter of pigs .... sold.
3. While they .... fishing I .... picking sea shells.
4. You .... playing while she .... studying.
5. The bride .... late arriving at the church and the groom .... worried.
6. There .... a fox in the chicken coop because there .... feathers scattered all over the place.
7. It .... snowing and we .... trapped in the forest.
8. Although the door .... closed the pigeons .... able to escape.
9. The ship .... sinking and the people .... panic-striken.
10. Mary .... happy when the cows .... milked.
11. We .... worried because our teacher .... seriously ill.
12. The man .... smiling but we .... afraid.
13. I .... reading while you .... writing.

Note: "**Were**" is always used after "**if**".
Examples: (i) **If I were** a rich man I would help the poor.
            (ii) **If Mary were** here she would play the guitar.

The Amazing Ants

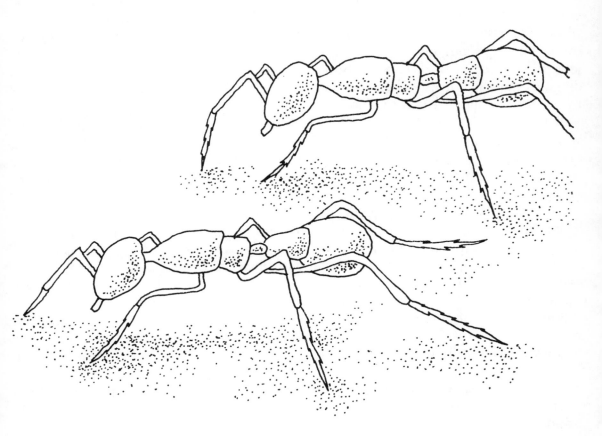

The queen ant lives in a large underground palace. Tiny tunnels lead into rest-rooms, storerooms and nursery play-centres for the baby ants. There is usually only one queen in each ant colony. She is bigger and stronger than the other ants. The female workers take care of the queen, whose chief *duty* is to lay eggs.

The young queen ant is born with wings. When she is strong enough, she leaves the nest and flies into the air. This is her marriage flight. The winged male ants eagerly follow her. She chooses the strongest one as her husband. After mating in flight, the male ant dies. The queen returns to build her new home. She tears off her wings as she no longer needs them.

She chooses a suitable site for her nest and digs a small tunnel in the ground. At the end of the tunnel she builds a private room. There she lays her tiny oval-shaped eggs. After 10-12 days they hatch out as larvae — fat, white, little grubs. They are soft and weak. The queen feeds them on unhatched eggs and a special juice from her own body. Gradually the soft grubs spin silken cocoons. When they *emerge* from the *cocoons*, they are full-grown ants.

The first ants out of the cocoons are all female workers. They dig their way out of the nest. At once, they set out in search of food to feed themselves and the queen mother. She enjoys watching her royal daughters busily at work. Now you know the meaning of the phrase "as busy as an ant". Some female nurses take care of the new-born ants. They feed them and keep them in the best rooms in the nest. At first the young ants are given easy jobs to do — removing dirt and rubbish from the nest, filling in broken-down walls and digging out new tunnels. When they are strong enough they join the main army of ants in the never-ending search for food.

When the colony of ants is strong enough the queen produces young princesses and winged male ants. These male ants or drones sit and wait for the flight of the young princesses. When the time comes the princesses leave the nest and marry. But many are eaten by birds, frogs, lizards, and snakes before they have a chance to build their new homes.

Though ants have poor eyesight, they have a wonderful sense of smell, taste and touch. They use their feelers or antennae to *communicate* with one another. It is fun to watch the busy little ants running about in zig-zag patterns and dragging bits of food back to the nest. They sweep the ground with their front teeth and *probe* for insects, sweet berries and seeds. Now and again one runs to the top of a blade of grass and waves her antennae at a brother or sister hurrying through the long grass.

Some species of ants capture greenflies or aphids. They keep them as "cows" in underground rooms. They feed them on leaves and on the stems of plants. When the ants want sweet milk from the greenflies, they simply *stroke* them with their feelers. Such clever farmers!

Ants bite people who annoy them or disturb their ant colony. Their bite is painful and sharp because they spit acid into the wound. You should watch an ant colony from a safe distance.

You can have your own ant colony in a tin box. Be sure to leave a hole at the top for the ants to run in and out. It would be wise to keep it at the bottom of the garden.

Look up the word in italics in the dictionary at the back of the book. Write down the meaning of each word.

Questions Answer the questions in sentence-form where possible.

1. Where does the queen live?
2. What is her duty in the nest?
3. What happens when she takes flight?
4. How are the larvae fed?
5. What kind of work do the female nurses do?
6. What creatures eat the ants?
7. How do ants talk to one another?
8. What food do they like to eat?
9. Why do they capture greenflies?
10. How do ants protect themselves?

A Farm Holiday

Write a story about a visit to a farm in the country.

Helpful words and ideas

.... invited to Uncle Jack's farm .... packed case .... train ....
met at the station .... tasty supper .... bed .... rose early ....
fed the chickens .... collected the eggs .... milking the cows ....
after dinner .... walk up the mountain .... wild flowers ....
fine view .... brought down the sheep and lambs .... clever sheepdog
.... drove sheep into their pens .... following day .... cleaned out the
stable .... fed the horse .... warm and sunny .... picnic
in the meadow .... gathered the hay .... strolled down to the beach
.... rolling waves .... explored rockpools .... late evening ....
sun sinking .... turf fire .... Uncle Jack's stories ....

Nature Notes For June

DOG-ROSE

HONEYSUCKLE

THE WOODS ARE FILLED WITH BIRD-SONG FROM SUNRISE TO SUNSET. SOON THE BIRDS WILL BE SILENT AGAIN.

IN THE FIELDS AND BY THE ROADSIDE MANY FLOWERS ENJOY THE LONG HOURS OF SUNSHINE.

LOOK OUT FOR BRIGHTLY-COLOURED BUTTERFLIES LIKE THE COMMON BLUE AND THE SMALL TORTOISESHELL

YOU CAN ALWAYS TELL A MOTH FROM A BUTTERFLY BY WHAT THEY DO WHEN THEY COME TO REST. A MOTH KEEPS ITS WINGS FLAT BUT A BUTTERFLY RAISES ITS WINGS ABOVE ITS BACK. DO YOU KNOW WHY?

THE SUNNY DAYS OF JUNE ARE HERE AND SOON THE LONG SUMMER HOLIDAY WILL START. TAKE THIS CHANCE TO FIND OUT AS MUCH AS YOU CAN ABOUT THE WONDERS OF NATURE. WHY NOT KEEP A NATURE DIARY OF ALL THE THINGS YOU SEE AND HEAR DURING YOUR HOLIDAY?

SMALL TORTOISESHELL

LEAVES HAVE GROWN ON ALL THE TREES AND SOME TREES ARE SHOWING BLOSSOMS TOO.

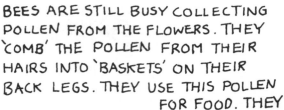

BEES ARE STILL BUSY COLLECTING POLLEN FROM THE FLOWERS. THEY 'COMB' THE POLLEN FROM THEIR HAIRS INTO 'BASKETS' ON THEIR BACK LEGS. THEY USE THIS POLLEN FOR FOOD. THEY ALSO TAKE NECTAR FROM THE FLOWERS, USING THEIR LONG TONGUES.

Nature Quiz

1. What can you hear in the woods?
2. What can you see in the fields?
3. When will the birds be silent again?
4. What is a 'common blue'?
5. How can you tell a moth from a butterfly?
6. Can you think of another difference between moths and butterflies?
7. What are some trees showing?
8. Why are the bees busy?
9. What does a bee have on its back legs?
10. How does a bee take nectar from flowers?
11. In what ways are bees useful to us?
12. Name the three months of summer.

↑ TONGUE

Adjectives (revision)

The **big, black** dog ran along the **narrow** lane.

The words **"Big"**, **"Black"**, and **"Narrow"** are descriptive words or adjectives. They tell us more about the dog and the lane.

(A) Write suitable adjectives for these sentences.

1. The .... child sat beside the .... fire.
2. The .... wolf escaped into the .... woods.
3. The .... balloon burst with a .... bang.
4. A .... beggar leaned against the .... door.
5. All the lambs were sold by the .... farmer.
6. The .... explorer sailed away in his .... ship.
7. The .... train rumbled into the .... station.
8. The field was covered with .... flowers.
9. We sat under a .... tree and had a .... picnic.
10. The fireman made his way through the .... smoke and flames.

(B) Write eight adjectives to describe each of these nouns.:
List: house, man, tiger, cliff. (If you need help, look for adjectives in the stories of this book.

	House	Man	Tiger	Cliff
1.	....	....	....	....
2.	....	....	....	....
3.	....	....	....	....
4.	....	....	....	....
5.	....	....	....	....
6.	....	....	....	....
7.	....	....	....	....
8.	....	....	....	....

(C) Write pairs of adjectives for each of these nouns.

Example: a **dark, stormy** night.

1. A .... , ... thief.
2. The .... , ... water.
3. The .... , ... desert.
4. A .... , ... puppy.
5. A .... , ... fox.
6. The .... , ... wall.
7. A .... , ... cake.
8. The .... , ... inventor.
9. The .... , ... saint.
10. A .... , ... cave.

Now write each one in an interesting sentence.

The Wee King

Iubhdán was king of the Wee Folk. On his birthday he held a great feast. The little people were given plates of roast mice and drank red wine from tiny glasses, the size of nuts. During the feast the king's strong man guarded the entrance of the fort. He was so strong a soldier that he could cut down a thistle with one blow of his sword.

At the end of the feast the king stood on a chair and spoke to the nobles.

"Does anyone know of a richer king that I?" he asked.

"We do not," replied the nobles.

"Does anyone know of a bigger army than mine?"

"We do not," they all shouted.

At that moment, a wee man named Eisirt began to laugh out loud. At once, there was silence in the great hall.

"Why do you laugh?" asked the Wee King.

"I know a country where there is one man who could destroy all your kingdom," replied Eisirt.

The king became very angry.

"*Seize* that man and throw him in prison," he said.

"Wait!" shouted Eisirt. "Give me a chance to prove that what I say is true. Let me have three days to go to Ireland and I shall return with a great warrior."

Iubhdán agreed to this. Eisirt travelled on his magic horse to the palace of King Fergus of Ulster. When the doorkeeper saw such a tiny man, he was surprised.

"Come in, little man," he said "King Fergus will be happy to see you."

Eisirt was brought before the court. He *bowed* to the king and told him his story. Then he played on a fairy harp and sang in such a sweet voice that the king promised him anything he wished in his kingdom.

"I only wish that Eda, your dwarf, return with me to Fairyland," said Eisirt. "In Fairyland, he shall be a giant."

"I would like to go there," said Eda.

"You may go," said King Fergus.

So, Eisirt and the smallest man in Ireland set out for Fairyland. When they arrived there, all the little people came out to see them. They thought the dwarf was a giant.

"Why have you brought this huge giant to kill us?" asked Iubhdán.

"He is the smallest man in Ireland," said Eisirt. "Now you know that I spoke the truth."

Iubhdán was very surprised and decided to visit Ulster, the Land of Giants.

So, he set out with Queen Bebo for Ireland. They rode on their fairy horse. It was early morning when they arrived before the palace gates. All the nobles were still asleep. Iubhdán and his wife crept under a big wooden door and found themselves in the kitchen. They were very hungry and climbed up to the top of a porridge pot. As Iubhdán leaned down to taste the porridge, he slipped and fell into the pot. His hands and feet got stuck in the thick porridge. Queen Bebo tried to lift him out with a big wooden spoon but she was not strong enough.

When the cook came to get the king's breakfast he pulled out Iubhdán and brought him and his queen before King Fergus. The king was delighted with the wee *couple*. He decided to keep them in the palace to sing and *entertain* himself and his nobles.

The fairies missed their king and queen very much. One day a small army of them arrived outside the palace of King Fergus. When he refused to free Iubhdán and Bebo, they cut down all his corn.

King Fergus still refused to free the Wee King and his wife. Next night the fairies stirred up the mud at the bottom of every well, lake and river in Ulster. Nobody was able to drink a drop of water. The King of Ulster was very angry and ordered Iubhdán to speak to his people.

"Tell them to make good the evil they have done or I shall kill Queen Bebo," said King Fergus.

Iubhdán went out and spoke to his people. "I cannot go with you without my wife Bebo. Unless you lift the evil spells you have cast over Ulster, she will be killed."

When the Wee Folk heard this they were very sad. They did as they were told and returned to Fairyland without their king and queen.

When the fairies had all gone, Iubhdán spoke to King Fergus.

"I beg you to let the queen and me go free. I shall give you a pair of magic shoes. When you wear them you can walk on land, on sea and under water."

"You may have your freedom," said Fergus.

The Wee King gave the magic shoes to Fergus. Then, he and Bebo rode off on their magic horse to Fairyland.

That was the last time that anybody saw the Wee Folk in Ulster.

Look up the words in italics in the dictionary at the back of the book. Write down the meaning of each word.

Questions

1. What was the name of the story?
2. Who was having a birthday feast?
3. What kind of food was served at the feast?
4. Why did Eisirt laugh at the king?
5. Why did he travel to Ulster?
6. What was the name of the king he met there?
7. Who returned to Fairyland with Eisirt?
8. Why were the fairies afraid of the dwarf?
9. How did Iubhdán and Bebo travel to Ulster?
10. What happened to the Wee King?
11. Why was Bebo not able to pull him out of the pot?
12. Why did King Fergus keep them in his palace?
13. What magic did the fairy army work?
14. Why did they return to Fairyland without their king?
15. How did Iubhdán get his freedom?

Creative Writing

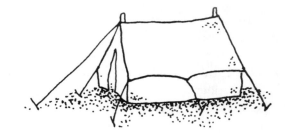

The Camp

1. Pretend you are on a camping holiday with your family. Write a story about your first evening.

Helpful words and ideas

.... hiking all day .... mountains ....
valleys .... late afternoon .... edge of a forest ....
cool, clear stream .... a good spot .... pitched the tent
.... collected firewood .... as hungry as a ....
cooked .... ate a delicious .... sun was setting
red sky .... tall pines .... crackling log fire ....
played the guitar .... moon appeared ....
twinkling star .... tired .... time for bed ....
crawled into .... hushed and still .... hoot of an owl
.... deep sleep ....

The Little People

2. Write a story about fairies or leprechauns.

.... on the hillside .... rainbow ....
followed .... across .... over ....
through .... a field of bright flowers .... a hawthorn bush
.... something flashed .... discovered a crock of gold
.... grabbed coins .... filled my pockets ....
heard a noise .... turned .... a tiny leprechaun ....
sitting on a .... he wore a .... jacket ....
trousers .... shoes .... seemed angry because ....
emptied my pockets .... dropped the coins .... ran
....

A Final Quiz

1. A tiny insect that bites.   A - -
2. This animal is called "Reynard".   F - -
3. A tree that is king of the forest.   O - -
4. A domestic animal that chews the cud.   C - -
5. A giant deer.   E - -
6. The meat of the pig.   P - - -
7. The early bird catches the ....   W - - -
8. The largest wild bird in Ireland.   S - - -
9. An animal in the story "Red Riding Hood".   W - - -
10. The king of the beasts.   L - - -
11. A huge, furry animal.   B - - -
12. An animal with antlers.   D - - -
13. This bird is king of the air.   E - - - -
14. An animal that lives in our rivers.   O - - - -
15. A bird with a red breast.   R - - - -
16. The plural of "goose".   G - - - -
17. The meat of the sheep.   M - - - - -
18. An Antarctic bird with a white waistcoat.   P - - - - - -
19. This animal has a very long neck.   G - - - - - -
20. This animal carries its young in its pouch.   K - - - - - - -
21. The fastest bird on land.   O - - - - - -
22. This insect lives in a hive.   H - - - - - - -

Garden Flowers

Write the names of the eight flowers.

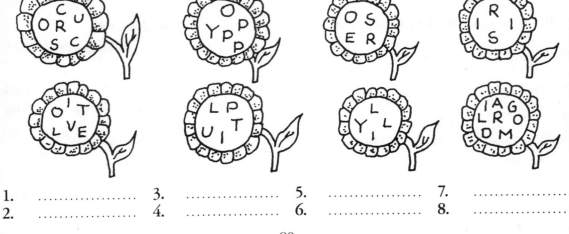

1. ....   3. ....   5. ....   7. ....
2. ....   4. ....   6. ....   8. ....

A Treasury of Words and Phrases

Descriptive Sounds

the babble of a stream
the blare of a trumpet
the beat of a drum
the blast of an explosion
the babbling of water
the boom of a gun
the chug of an engine
the clang of a bell
the clatter of hooves
the crack of a whip
the creak of a hinge
the crinkle of paper
the chime of a clock
the clink of a coin
the gurgle of a drain-pipe
the grinding of brakes
the hissing of steam
the hoot of a horn
the hubbub of voices
the jingle of coins
the lapping of water
the pitter-patter of raindrops
the ping of a bullet
the popping of corks
the rattle of dishes
the rasp of a file
the rumble of a train
the rush of feet
the rustling of leaves
the screech of brakes
the sighing of the wind
the swish of skirts
the sizzling of sausages
the shuffling of feet
the tramp of feet
the tick of a clock
the twang of a bow
the thunder of hooves
the wail of a siren
the whirring of wings

Sounds and Movements of Birds

the crow caws and flaps her wings
the eagle screams and swoops
the hen cackles and struts
the lark sings and soars
the owl hoots and flits
the parrot screeches and flits
the pigeon coos and flutters
the seagull screams and glides
the sparrow chirps and hops
the swallow twitters and dives
the turkey gobbles and struts
the robin chirps and hops
the duck quacks and waddles
the wren warbles and hops

Sounds and Movements of Domestic Animals

the horse neighs and gallops
the lamb bleats and frisks
the pig grunts and trots
the dog barks and runs
the cow lows and wanders
the cat purrs and steals
the bull bellows and charges
the donkey brays and jogs

Sounds and Movements of Wild Animals

the lion roars and prowls
the bear growls and lumbers
the elephant trumpets and ambles
the hyena screams and prowls
the monkey chatters and climbs
the rabbit squeals and leaps
the wolf howls and lopes
the mouse squeaks and scampers
the gorilla gibbers and swings

Masculine and Feminine of Nouns

prince	princess	giant	giantess
king	queen	brave	squaw
earl	countess	mayor	mayoress
emperor	empress	instructor	instructress
host	hostess	grandfather	grandmother
duke	duchess	manservant	maidservant
count	countess	postman	postwoman
baron	baroness	author	authoress
peer	peeress	heir	heiress
prophet	prophetess	traitor	traitress
wizard	witch	enchanter	enchantress
father	mother	deacon	deaconess
hero	heroine	beau	belle
husband	wife	shepherd	shepherdess
lad	lass	tailor	tailoress
gentleman	lady	warder	wardress
brother	sister		
tutor	governess	**Animals**	
lord	lady	colt	filly
master	mistress	buck rabbit	doe rabbit
nephew	niece	bull	cow
son	daughter	gander	goose
sir	madam	steer	heifer
man	woman	dog	bitch
landlord	landlady	boar	sow
headmaster	headmistress	cock	hen
bridegroom	bride	stag	hind
bachelor	spinster	fox	vixen
widower	widow	ram	ewe
actor	actress	billy goat	nanny goat
abbot	abbess	cock sparrow	hen sparrow
monk	nun	bullock	heifer
priest	priestess	tiger	tigress
waiter	waitress	lion	lioness
manager	manageress	bull seal	cow seal
negro	negress	leopard	leopardess
poet	poetess	tom-cat	tabby cat
god	goddess	he-wolf	she-wolf
stepfather	stepmother	drake	duck
steward	stewardess	stallion	mare

Collective Words

a brood of chickens
a gaggle of geese
a flock of geese
a paddling of ducks
a herd of cattle
a herd of antelope
a flock of birds
a flock of sheep
a swarm of bees
a swarm of insects
a hive of bees
a team of horses
a string of horses
a team of oxen
a pride of lions
a troop of monkeys
a herd of buffaloes
a nest of rabbits
a nest of mice
a pack of hounds
a pack of wolves
a down of hares
a fall of woodcock
a plague of locusts
a kennel of dogs
a herd of elephants
a wisp of snipe
a flight of doves
a plague of insects
a shoal of herring
a school of whales
a tribe of goats
a sloth of bears
a skulk of foxes
a pride of lions
a flight of swallows
a barren of mules
a covey of grouse
a litter of pups
a litter of cubs
a flock of geese

Similes

as sly as a fox
as tender as a chicken
as slow as a tortoise
as slow as a snail
as meek as a lamb
as brave as a lion
as proud as a peacock
as busy as a bee
as busy as an ant
as blind as a bat
as playful as a kitten
as red as a turkey-cock
as fat as a pig
as strong as a horse
as strong as an ox
as happy as a lark
as mad as a March hare
as wise as an owl
as swift as a deer
as gentle as a lamb
as frisky as a lamb
as fierce as a lion
as slippery as an eel
as agile as a monkey
as hungry as a wolf
as graceful as a swan
as obstinate as a mule
as stubborn as a mule
as timid as a rabbit
as hairy as a gorilla
as sure-footed as a goat
as silly as a sheep
as fast as a hare
as brown as a berry
as sweet as honey
as white as snow
as fresh as a daisy
as purple as the heather
as green as grass
as sturdy as an oak
as cold as ice

Dictionary

abandon: to give up, to desert.
acquire: to get something.
adventure: an exciting experience.
aloft: high up.
ancient: of times long past.
armour: a cover worn for protection in fighting.
arouse: to stir into action.

bait: food which is used to try to catch an animal or fish.
bargain: good value.
batch: a group, or collection.
beam: (1) a ray of light.
            (2) a long piece of timber.
blubber: fat.
board: to enter a ship.
boulder: a large rock.
bow: to bend down or kneel.

carcass: dead body of an animal.
cargo: load (a ship's load)
carriage: a four-wheeled vehicle.
chieftain: a leader of a tribe or clan.
clumsy: awkward in movement.
cocoon: silky case spun by insect.
communicate: to pass messages.
competition: contest.
couple: pair.
crafty: clever, cunning.
creature: a living thing.
cunning: clever (but clever in a selfish way).

deceive: mislead.
deck: a floor or platform on a ship.
destination: the place for which a person or thing is headed.
develop: to grow.
devour: eat quickly/greedily.
diet: the kind of food on which a person or animal lives.

digested: eaten.
droplets: small drops.
duty: work, or what a person ought to do

emerge: come out into view.
enlarge: make bigger.
entertain: to amuse.
excellent: very good.
exchange: swap.
expedition: a journey for a definite purpose.
exposed: uncovered.

fashion: shape.
funnel: a tube which is wide at the top and narrow at the end (used for pouring liquid into a small opening).

gallant: brave.
galloped: ran rapidly.
gloomy: dark.
glossy: shiny.
glowing: shining.
grant: give, allow to have.
grove: a small wood.

immediately: without delay, straightaway
impression: idea or notion.

keen: (1) sharp or strong,
         (2) eager.

kilometre: a thousand metres.

lest: for fear that.

magnificent: brilliant, splendid.
mankind: the human race.
marble: a very hard rock (used in building and statues)
meadow: a piece of grassland used for hay

migrate: come and go with the seasons.
morsel: small piece.
musician: a maker of music.
mute: silent, without speech.

nestling: a very young bird.

nobles: people of high class.

occupy: live in.
oval: egg-shaped.

pattern: a colourful design or shape.
perch: (of a bird) to rest on.
plain: of land which is level.
plead: beg.
pluck: pull at; pick.
plumage: a bird's feathers.
plump: fat.
plunge: dive into.
pounce: swoop, come down suddenly.
probe: explore or examine.
propeller: the turning blades which drive a ship or plane forward.
protect: keep safe.

rear: (1) stand upright on hind legs.
     (2) bring up. (e.g. rear a family)
reflect: to throw back light, heat or sound.
region: area or district.
regular: constant, (or the same thing at the same time daily).
rejoice: be glad.
reply: answer.
rhythm: a steady beat.
roam: wander.

sapling: a young tree.
scamper: run like a frightened animal.
scan: examine by sight.
secrete: store liquid.
seize: grab.
select: choose.

shallow: not deep.
shield: protect.
shrub: a woody plant which is smaller than a tree.
sift: pass through a sieve.
sieve: used in cooking to separate flour — the small fine particles only pass through the sieve.
sinews: join muscles to bones.
slender: slim.
slither: slide.
snout: nose.
solitary: only, alone.
spare: to pardon.
stalk: (1) creep up behind to kill an animal.
     (2) the stem of a plant.
stroke: rub gently.
stubby: short and thick and strong.
sturdy: strong.
succeed: (1) follow.
     (2) avoid failure.
suction: sucking.
surface: the outside of a thing.

talons: claws of a bird.
territory: land.
tint: a weak colour.
thud: a dull sound made when an object falls.
transparent: something that can be seen through.
trespass: enter another person's property without permission.

unsteady: shaky.

valley: a low area between hills.
vanish: disappear.
variety: a collection of unlike things.
venture: attempt.
visible: can be seen.
weir: a dam or barrier across a river.
widow: a woman whose husband has died.